Ways of the Bird

THE PERENNIAL CYCLE OF BIRD LIFE

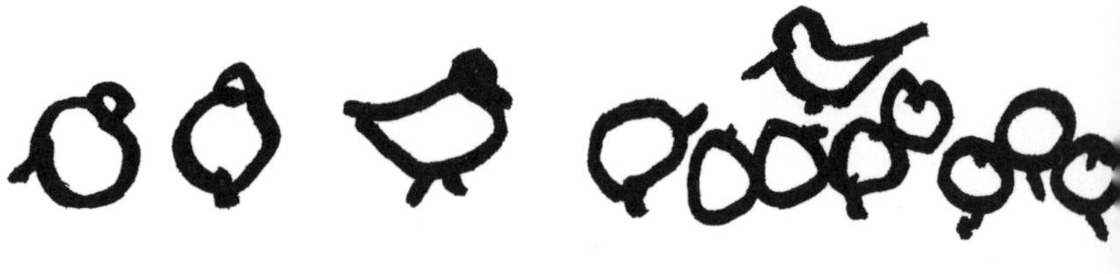

Ways of the Bird

SARITA VAN VLECK

LYONS & BURFORD, PUBLISHERS

Printed in the United States of America

10 9 8 7 6 5 4 3 2 1

Library of Congress Cataloging-in-Publication Data

Van Vleck, Sarita.
    [Growing wings]
    Ways of the bird : a naturalist's guide to bird behavior / Sarita
    Van Vleck.
        p.   cm.
    Originally published: Growing wings. Dublin, N.H. : W.L. Bauhan,
1977.
    Includes bibliographical references (p. 133) and index.
    ISBN 1-55821-223-X
    1. Birds—Behavior.   I. Title.
QL698.3.V3   1993
598.251—dc20   92-44771
                                                          CIP

This book is dedicated

to

those who cared for me

"in the nest,"

and those who lured me

out of it

Preface

Several thousand species of birds throughout the world struggle for existence in an essentially hostile environment. The multitude of ways they have evolved to cope with the problems of individual survival and of reproduction furnish some of the most exciting and dramatic stories to be found. *Ways of the Bird* presents us with some of this excitement and drama. Moreover, it does not sacrifice accuracy for sensationalism—a fault with most such attempts to present the facts of nature to the layman.

Sarita Van Vleck has skillfully presented an accurate account of the yearly struggle for survival and reproduction while preserving its essential drama. She has painted her picture with broad strokes but has liberally used accurate, specific examples to illustrate her points.

The reader will be impressed by the basic similarity between problems facing us and those facing birds in the daily struggle for existence. Men and birds are both vertebrate animals. They share many fundamental anatomical, physiological, and behavioral features. The things we learn about other animals, including birds, inevitably help us to increase knowledge of ourselves. This is particularly true in the field of animal behavior. Our continued survival as a species in this day of nuclear potential may very well depend on the speedy acquisition of a much deeper understanding of our own behavior.

This book, therefore, not only presents the reader with the enjoyment derived from feeling something of the excitement and drama of the lives of birds along with the discovery that we have much in common with them, but also with the realization that the kinds of information included in these pages helps to understand ourselves better.

Dr. William C. Dilger
CORNELL UNIVERSITY

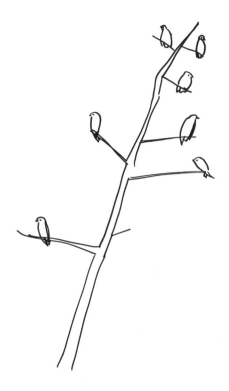

Foreword to the New Edition

Since 1963 when this book was first published under the title *Growing Wings*, an abundance of new information has flowed into ornithological literature. Because the facts as originally published have borne the test of time—and to avoid altering the character of the original work—I have left the text unchanged except for a few minor corrections. Some important additions, however, have been included in the new edition: an Appendix, in which I report a few recent findings of general interest; a new "Sources and Recommended Reading" list for a more comprehensive understanding of ongoing research; and—perhaps most useful of all to the reader—a full index (omitted from earlier editions) has been compiled and included here. The new index and selected bibliography will contribute greatly to the practical value of the book and to the reader's enjoyment.

When the book was first published there existed, beyond the numerous texts and field guides, a dearth of ornithological literature for the layman. For two years previously I had studied with increasing fascination dozens of books and hundreds of papers as part of my research for museum exhibits, but it was not until I had completed my work that I saw in retrospect the need for a "popular" book. By writing this book I could share with others some of what I had learned, knowledge that helped me understand, above all, where I fit into the natural scheme and how to behave within it.

The original manuscript was read for accuracy by three professional ornithologists to whom thanks are long overdue: Dean Amadon of the American Museum of Natural History, William Dilger of Cornell, and the late William Vogt, then with the Conservation Foundation. In spite of this careful combing several readers found "inaccuracies," most particularly the "myth" of the swansong. For their information I have included in the new appendix a passage from the sources.

Ways of the Bird is now reissued in paperback for the many enthusiastic old friends who have requested it, and for new readers who may wish to share what I hope will be an exciting learning experience in the field of ethology and beyond . . . into the miraculous lives we have been conditioned to regard as alien to our own.

As wild bird populations dwindle before the steady advance of "people birds"—crows, pigeons, starlings, house sparrows—the time is past when we can afford to view a wild organism as essentially different from ourselves and therefore subject to a different set of rules. Ecological studies demonstrate continuously that we are bound together in the "web of life"; our differences are superficial while our similarities turn out to be basic. Certainly in their need for adequate shelter, food, air and living space, man and bird are one.

Man's gift for manipulating his environment is universally evident. Less apparent to us is the "light" of nature eclipsed by the "bushel basket" of Man's ignorant and fearful domination. Having slipped from beneath that "bushel basket," I feel I have achieved in large measure what one can only wish to share with others, the silent serenity of flight . . .

Sarita Van Vleck

Contents

List of Illustrations

Then the Great Crane rose, stretched his neck three times, and said: sruṅ dgos, which means, one must observe.

The Buddha's Law Among the Birds

Ways of the Bird

I The Bird Year

Quietly and unnoticed, dormant winter has evolved into wakening spring. The flaming April sun slips silently into the aquamarine Gulf of Mexico, leaving the glowing sandstrip to cool under the lowering dampness. Defining the length of the beach are scattered groups of plump shorebirds ready to move north.

One flock of several hundred Dunlins, or Red-backed Sandpipers, are standing apart from the toylike Sanderlings with whom they usually associate. All around them are solitary Black-bellied Plovers warily glancing around between pokes at the sand. Down the beach is a tight group of rust-breasted Knots, the birds trotting with heads held high, in and out among their friends who are eating and resting. Few of them dare part from the flock to investigate the unknown as Dunlins do.

At first glance the Dunlins appear as a pack of mice on stilts. Their cocoa-brown backs are gradually filling in with the summer russet, while their white bellies are spotted with black feathers, as though they had alighted momentarily in tar. Most of them are excited and alert. Moving with heavy deliberation this way and that, they jab their decurved bills into the snapping sand near the low tide's edge. One pulls out a threadlike marine worm and turns to run up the beach away from his less fortunate friends who chase him. He stops and swallows an inch of worm, then runs ahead to stop again, until the worm is down and everyone returns to the edge to find more worms. Others restlessly talk among themselves and draw fresh flight feathers through their bills, putting the interlocking barbs in place. Those who have finished feeding stand vacantly on two legs, pivoting from side to side. A few rest first on one leg, then on the other, scurrying short distances between shifts. Some stand peacefully on one foot with their soft gray heads tucked under their wings, sound asleep for the moment.

The tide turns to flood the beach once more. The air is still. The birds are waiting, hundreds of bills impatiently marking all points of the compass at once. Softly the south wind whispers across the water. Scarcely perceptible at first, it finally reaches the shore to brush the weightless cheeks of the flock who face it. A ripple moves across their spread of backs. Suddenly, as if released from a trap, the leaderless Red-backs spring up and forward as one, flashing white as they dart out over the Gulf, and in a wide sweeping arc disappear in the dusk to the north. Leaving on the beach an irregular expanse of well-defined three-toed footprints, all jumbled together, denoting activity, with no trail leading away.

This isolated event is the opening scene in the play of a bird year. The year is a continuous cycle whose motivating theme is the perpetuation of bird life. It has its passionate climax in the heat of summer and its depleted denouement in the chill of winter. It is a tragicomedy whose development takes place within the narrow confines of instinct, and whose scenes afford most humans the opportunity of seeing their animal natures at a distance, reminding the thoughtful that from the scaly reptile rose both the feathered bird and the hair-covered mammal.

The bird year consists of the four seasons that regulate nature—spring, summer, fall, and winter. Each period has its counterpart in the ordinary twenty-four-hour day, spring in sunrise, summer in noonday, fall in sunset, and winter in night.

Birds spend the year in much the same way as people do, responding to the weather. In spring they move from the winter home to the summer, stopping along the way for food and rest. During the summer they are frantically raising their young. Through fall the birds leisurely return with their new members to the winter homes. All winter they rest and feed at popular resorts, building up energy reserves to carry them through the following year and the next reproductive cycle. Most of this they do by instinct.

Webster defines instinct as "a tendency to actions which lead to the attainment of some goal natural to the species."

The natural goal of most species is survival. Whereas man can ponder over whether or not he wishes to survive and then act according to his decision, birds have no choice in the matter. They must survive as individuals and as a group.

During most of the year each bird is concerned with his own survival, so that when he is approached he instinctively makes haste to escape. As the nesting season progresses, the goal is broadened to survival of the species. Then a bird will risk, but not intentionally sacrifice, its life to save its young. Which of the two goals prevails depends on the season, since most birds react to weather changes in the same way.

In late winter when the days grow longer, every bird undergoes a gradual but radical change which eventually guides most healthy adults into the holey confines of the nuptial net. The initial changes are internal and unseeable.

Increasing daylight stimulates the outpouring of gonadotropic* hormones by the pituitary gland. These are extremely potent substances which are carried by the bloodstream to remote parts of the

* Literally gonad-changing, from the Greek *tropi*, to change.

body—target organs—where they step up the rate of cell activity. They effect the growth of sex cells and the production of the gonadal hormones. The gonadal hormones in turn activate the breeding cycle, stimulating the development of useful physiological assets such as seductive mating plumage, and dictating how one bird shall respond to another.

These changes are effected over a period of weeks. So although winter is popularly considered to be a dull gray period of sleep, it is to the contrary a time of mysterious hormonal activity when each organism is preparing for its climactic role in the simple seductions of springtime.

II Spring Migration

One chilly damp night somewhere north of the south, the earth is newly free of the winter frost and the temperature averages thirty-five degrees.

In the bottom of its burrow a hungry earthworm works its way free of the hibernation ball and wends its way to the surface. It unplugs the entrance and crawls partway out into the black dewy night. Slowly the night crawler devours the moist organisms of decay, casting the spoils around the rim of its burrow. The sun rises and a Robin drops down to feed. He pounces on the ill-fated worm and snatches it in his bill. Leaning backward he pulls steadily until the reluctant victim has been stretched full length out of its burrow, gulps it down, and cocks his eye for another late worm.

Thus the Robins move north as earthworms appear, migrating like the Canada Geese along the leading edge of spring.

Where tropical birds can remain in their equatorial homes and breed almost the year round, most birds, for reasons unknown, stage mass migrations in spring and fall as part of their breeding cycle. Just how they fly from one small area to another with such accuracy has fascinated men for centuries.

Recent experiments have demonstrated that some birds orient themselves according to the sun or stars. In 1949 Common Starlings in an indoor aviary were trained to seek food in a station at compass point north. This station was one of twelve whose positions were regularly changed. On sunny days the birds had no difficulty locating their northerly food, but on cloudy days they were completely confused. Another experiment involved finding food at a compass point in a room with six small windows. The starlings found it easily until the last window was closed and the precious sun shut off from view. This suggested that daytime migrants navigate by the sun.

To discover the secret of nocturnal migrants, other experiments were carried out in 1956. Warblers were hatched and reared in soundproof boxes out of contact with other birds. In the fall they flitted about in their boxes for the duration of the normal migratory flight to Africa, then resumed their usual sleeping habits. Later the birds were put into a cage so they could see the night sky. On clear nights during migration time they positioned themselves in directions that were accurate for the various species. On cloudy nights their direction-finding was nil.

Finally some of these bewildered warblers were taken inside the Bremen Planetarium where they were set free under a German "sky." One bird flying to Egypt suddenly found himself relocated to Siberia. After a minute of doubtful hesitation, the warbler resumed its somewhat labored trip by heading back to the migration route along which its wild relatives presumably were traveling.

Other feats are less easily explained. On the Bering Sea some members of a survey were on a steamship heading through fog for an island colonized by murres. While the ship was navigating according to compass and chart, flocks of murres emerged from the fog astern, passed the ship, and disappeared into the gray ahead, unencumbered by instruments.

Another ploy is the ability of some young shorebirds, deserted by their parents when ten days old, to migrate from the Arctic to the Argentine where they rejoin the adults for the winter—as though they had flown the route many times before.

Migration movements are followed by the simple technique of bird-banding which is done by qualified persons the world over. Some birds are banded while still in the nest. Others are trapped momentarily while a band is placed on the leg. The number, date, and locale of each banding is sent to the United States Fish and Wildlife Service in Washington by the bander. When the bird is recovered, the finder sends the appropriate data to Washington, according to directions on the band itself. There the facts are correlated, the approximate route of movement determined, and the time it took to traverse the distance estimated.

There are three types of migrations: altitudinal, longitudinal, and latitudinal. Movements of the first type take place mainly in the West where jays, juncos, chickadees, and nuthatches move down from their wind-lashed mountaintops to the lower valleys for the winter, and fly back up for the summer. Longitudinal migrations occur when birds such as the Redhead Duck leave the eastern wintering area and fly to the West for the nesting season. Latitudinal migration consists of mass bird movements from south to north and back again in the fall. Of the three types this is the best known because it flows over everyone's rooftop at one time or another.

Spring migration usually coincides with the reawakening of the various life-forms in the north. Myriad organisms awaken to perpetuate their kinds—each to serve as food for stronger kinds, each to form a link in what is known as the food chain. Each sleeping animal and plant revives as the mercury reaches a certain level.

Birds migrate with the temperature that frees their food supply from the clutches of winter. In February, New Jersey fields and lakes are thawing sufficiently to supply migrating Pintails with seeds.

In March, with the temperature climbing through the thirties, Redwings move with their rasping chatter over the fresh marshes, gleaning the seeds relinquished by receding snows. Canada Geese feed on the seeds and sprouts of thawing upland pastures en route to the thawing northern lake shores. Robins put pressure on the lowly earthworm. In April and May the mercury soars to the forties and fifties, unleashing clouds of aerial insects which bring on swifts and swallows. Leaves unfold and insects emerge to provide food for the waves of wood warblers, thrushes, and vireos who roll by in May. At the end of the month, flowers unsheath, disclosing their insect-filled reservoirs of nectar to newly arrived Ruby-throated Hummingbirds.

Not all birds need, or are able, to migrate. Many, including members of typical migratory species, remain behind the others and form resident populations where they winter. Some individuals are unable to migrate because of physical unfitness. A prerequisite to migrating in spring is the strong and plump condition of the migrant. If a bird is not ready to undertake the journey, he will not feel the migration impulse when the others do, and will stay put.

Though the reappearance of food usually coincides with the arrival of the migrants, migrations are actually set off by light increase and weather changes. The general restlessness that precedes migrations starts with the onset of hormonal activity, allows an increase in

the rate of feeding, and results accordingly in the necessary accumulation of fat. When the birds have reached a certain pitch of readiness, a change in weather will release them. A wind shift from southwest clockwise to the south, bringing with it low pressure and rising temperatures, generally initiates the spring migration. The flight continues until a high-pressure cold front dams up the flow of the south wind and floods the woods with birds. The migrants are earthbound until the dam breaks and warm weather again pushes them on their way. During such floods, the birds are usually tired, hungry, and unwary with fatigue, making them easy subjects for all observers.

Migratory movements occur night and day, depending on the bird's feeding habits as well as his ability to escape flying predators.

Nocturnal migrants are generally the smaller birds who depend on darkness for concealment, who can find food only in daylight, and who must eat often. Wood warblers, thrushes, vireos, orioles, tyrant flycatchers, some sparrows, rails, and most shorebirds are such migrants. Flying by night they recuperate by day, many foraging northward as they feed.

Radar has shown that most night-fliers fly between one thousand and three thousand feet altitude in the hours from 8:00 P.M. to midnight, and four to six in the morning. It seems likely that many of them ride the low-level nocturnal jets occurring on clear nights between one and two thousand feet. These jets reach peak speeds of fifty to eighty miles per hour between sunset and midnight, and die in the early morning, giving some birds the opportunity of a smooth effortless journey north.

Diurnal migrants, those who fly during the day, include the loons, gulls and terns, pelicans, cranes, hawks, hummingbirds, swallows, swifts, and nighthawks. The larger birds are able to fly for hours without refueling and have few enemies, where the smaller ones feed as they travel and usually outmaneuver any attackers.

A few birds migrate day or night. Generally they are the wading and swimming birds whose feeding on aquatic plants and insects is unrelated to darkness, and who escape their enemies by means other than concealment.

Typically, small birds coming from South America fly directly over the Caribbean to the Gulf States, their premigratory fat deposition lasting them through continuous flights of six hundred miles or thirty-six hours, perhaps more. Those who depend on insects taken in flight usually fly the overland route through Mexico. Consequently the northward wave of birds rolls into the United States in a front that extends from one shore to the other.

Though normal migrating altitude is under five thousand feet, geese have been recorded at twenty-nine thousand over the Himalayas, cranes at thirteen thousand above the English Channel, and even very small songbirds were "heard" by radar at twenty-one thousand feet on a British night in September. On cloudy days the birds fly beneath the clouds, avoiding the turbulent interiors as airline pilots try to.

Flight speeds vary with the normal flight habits of the birds. Songbirds fly twenty-five miles per hour on the average, while waterfowl and plovers reach fifty. Dunlins have been seen at fifteen hundred feet flying an estimated 110 mph, undoubtedly using a strong tail wind. Canada Geese move easily at sixty, but speed seems lost on those individuals who sometimes prefer to walk a quarter of a mile rather than fly.

With the exception of transoceanic routes, most flights are slow in their rate of advancement. Small landbirds usually fly only a few hours each night, which limits their distance to the forty miles typical of the Robin advancing with spring.

The Blackpoll Warbler is a fast erratic nocturnal migrant who takes four weeks to go from South America to the Alaska-Newfoundland nesting limit. From April 30 to May 10 the Blackpolls average thirty miles a day. But crossing Canada during the last week they cover two hundred miles a day as social synchrony intensifies.

The Cliff Swallow is a slow steady diurnal migrant who leaves South America four weeks earlier than the sea-crossing warbler, and slowly wends its way up through Central America and Mexico. Its circuitous overland route allows it to feed as it swoops through the insectful air, flying up a mileage that well belittles the extra two thousand land miles. In all, the swallow takes twice as long to migrate as the warbler.

How rapidly the birds advance depends partly on the time of year they fly. Those who travel in February and March are constantly beset by the seesaw weather of early spring. One setback occurred when 750,000 Lapland Longspurs were forced down by a sudden March snowstorm over a lake in Minnesota. The next day their white bodies were found encased by ice over an area of two square miles.

Robins, crows, and flickers are pre-April migrants who, from first to last, take fifty to eighty days to pass through New Jersey, where May migrants such as the American Redstart go through in twenty to thirty days. The Philadelphia Vireo shoots by in the middle week of May and the Mourning Warbler can be seen during the final week. Certain individual warblers, vireos, and orioles can be expected to arrive in a specific neighborhood on about the same day year after year. Such precise transits are possible only with the settled weather of May.

Spring arrival dates for any one species can be scattered or concentrated. At Ithaca, New York, a bird study was carried out on the boisterous Redwinged Blackbird. The vagrant Redwings were done with aimless wandering and returned in February and March, arriving first the way gypsies do at country fairs. Later in March both migrants and resident males appeared. Their female complements came in April, to be followed in May and June by the less determined, irresponsible immatures. The dates cover the entire migration span, marking Redwings as a hardy and adaptable species. The order in which they arrived seems to be characteristic of most songbirds. More concentrated arrivals are typical of Canada Geese who travel as families and are less victimized by weather changes. They usually appear during the March-April transition.

The Arctic is the northern terminus for long-distance migrants, the majority of whom converge on the thawing tundra during the last two weeks of May—days before the first leaves emerge, two months before the hottest days occur. They arrive still bearing the twenty percent excess of migratory fat. The extra weight carries the overactive males through their courtship when some take no time to eat, and the females through incubation. All birds seem to thin down once the young hatch.

Upon arrival, most of the birds are still in migratory flocks. Within hours the flocks have broken down into myriad individuals bent on family matters. The Arctic nesting season is short, the spring temperatures are extreme, and the food supply inconstant. These rigid conditions compel the birds to act in concert regarding time and place to nest. The transitions between stages of the reproductive cycle seem to be shorter, and the usually lengthy period of competition for mates and nest sites is abbreviated.

The average time from the day of arrival to the laying of the first egg, usually during the first week of June, is seventeen days. Once the laying starts, the birds proceed, more or less in unison, from one stage to the next so that by the end of July most songbird young are flying.

Then family ties disintegrate, incubating mothers desert their eggs or young willy-nilly, and most individuals rejoin flocks preparatory to the trip south.

No small wonder that most birds lead a more leisurely life south of the tundra and further removed from urgency.

III Territory

A confident Brown Thrasher darts across the yard, spreads wide his ample wings and tail, and swoops deftly down into the glistening emerald top of a fruit tree. There he perches, slowly expanding his splendid brown-and-white striped chest, holding his head high to display the striking white throat. For a moment he is the uncontested star of the garden.

Suddenly from the dark depths of a neighboring bush comes a loud harsh *tch!* The cavalier looks first confused, then alarmed. He depresses his expanded feathers, flicks his tail, and looks nervously about. He opens his long bill and emits a gulping *chirrup* in reply. Again comes the *tch!* very loud and brusque. The thrasher repeats his performance for the invisible adversary. The warnings become more frequent and persistent.

Upset by the presence of settled competition, the hero waxes wild-eyed. Flicking his tail constantly and pivoting in all directions seeking his opponent, he opens his bill and no sound comes out. He shimmies silently. The warnings are coming every second. With his initial display shattered, the defeated thrasher flattens his tail and flies over the top of the tree and out of sight in hasty silence.

The owner of that territory has successfully ousted the intruder with a minimum of effort and exposure.

As male migrants near their nesting grounds, they gradually change from gay, sociable companions into highly competitive rivals. The flocks break up and the members separate in order to compete for mates, each male finding a piece of property to claim as his territory, many returning to the same holding as in years past.

A territory is any area defended by a bird and used by him for the support of himself or his family. It makes food-gathering for the young somewhat easier in many cases, and it helps assure the even distribution of birds over the available nesting areas. A territory provides a bird with a place to hide and a home to protect where courting, mating, and usually nesting can be carried on in stimulating fashion, for encounters between the owners and trespassers may invigorate the breeding behavior of all concerned.

There are several types of territories. One covers only several square yards and is used by polygamous males as a place to which the females come for mating. Such is the display area of the European Ruff and the prairie chickens of our Midwest.

The American Woodcock male has two territories that he uses for day and night. The diurnal territory covers about 1250 square yards of woods in which the male spends his days quietly feeding. At night he moves to his fifty square feet of a nearby open area where he performs his courtship flights for visiting females. Both territories are likely to have moist areas for feeding which may aid in the gathering of the sexes. Like some other polygamous birds, the hen has her own nesting territory which she maintains usually within half a mile of the male.

Another small territory is the loafing bar which most ducks hold so that their mates may come there between duties at the nest, the uninterested drakes usually being ignorant of the nest's whereabouts.

The smallest territories are found among birds who nest in colonies, such as gulls, herons, and Cliff Swallows. These may cover a square foot or two and are used for courtship, copulation, and nesting. Among the murres, Gannets, and other cliff-dwelling seabirds where space comes at a premium, the size of a territory is usually determined by the length of the bird's bill and his ability to use it on all fronts at once. Colonial nesters use a common feeding ground, such as the ocean, which eliminates the necessity for larger territories.

Geese, hawks, and most other birds are more isolated nesters who need a larger territory to fulfill their needs. In addition to sites for courting, mating, and nesting their territories must often supply enough food for the voracious appetites of the young. Although chickadees, some hawks, Robins, Tree Swallows, and waxwings seem to have neutral feeding areas, the vast majority of birds feed in the proximity of their territorial boundaries, some within and some without. The size of these areas depends largely on the availability of food. Hawks hunt but do not defend an area of several square miles. Eastern Meadowlarks need about seven acres. Small birds, such as warblers, survive on an acre or less. In years of insect infestation their territories shrink to a fraction of the usual.

Redwing territories may be large or small, depending on how many males are sharing the marsh, and how much food is taken from within the boundaries. In one area the average size may be nine thousand square feet, and in another it may be one third of that. One opportunistic male steadily increased his holdings over five years from 1326 square feet to 5350.

Some of the weaverbirds of Africa establish territories whose size seems to be unrelated to the availability of food. Within one genus, one species has a large territory no matter how many males are present, while another can get along on a small one. The large one may vary from six hundred to twelve hundred square yards and will house no more than three females at once. The small one may be ten square yards or less and contain up to five nesting hens who may produce eight families.

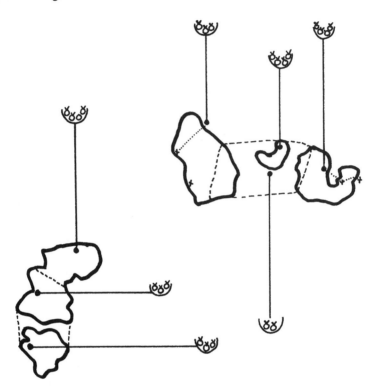

ISLAND TERRITORIES OF
THIRTEEN REDWINGS.

--- BOUNDARIES

× DESERTED NESTS
(eggs or young destroyed)

♂ YOUNG

O INFERTILE EGGS

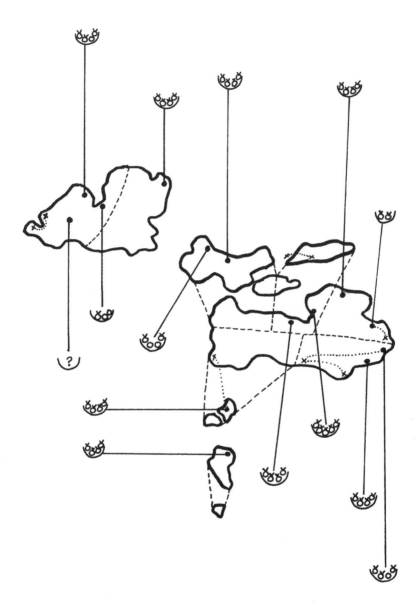

The requisites of a bird's life help determine the location of a territory. The Redwing's nest is ordinarily built in low waterside bushes or emergent vegetation, but can be found anywhere between the ground and the top of a tree twenty feet high. Usually every territory has a tree from which the bird can display his ownership. Although the nest site varies, the nest must be made of grasses, and iris or cattail reeds, and the basket chinks closed with peat, rotted wood, or mud. The main food items are caddisflies and mayflies, which hatch and live in aquatic environments. With life centered around a wet habitat, the Redwing would be unlikely to nest in its absence. Although some individuals do nest on the uplands, the success of marsh-nesters is higher.

The Eastern Meadowlark usually chooses a moist territory in a meadow with abundant grass matting in which the grassy cave nest can be formed. The preferred food consists of meadow insects, such as grasshoppers, which are most abundant in open areas. The territory must also include a fencepost or other vantage point from which the male can whistle and display his black-banded egg-yellow front. The meadowlark's spasmodic mode of flight with the straight course pursued is best suited to an open field, as the bird is less skilled at darting in and out among trees and twigs. Consequently he is rarely seen in the woods.

Territorial boundaries are vague to the human eye, but each bird has a clear idea of where his territory begins and ends. The point is to convey the same picture to his competitors.

The defense of a territory is based on the rule that birds of kinds different from the owner usually may pass through his territory as they please, or even nest there, but males of the same kind are competitors and must stay off. As a result, pairs of Robins, Eastern King-birds, Orchard Orioles, and Warbling Vireos can be found nesting together in the same tree. Mockingbirds are among the exceptions who are belligerent toward anyone who passes through their domain. Redwings are intolerant of Purple Grackles and Long-billed Marsh Wrens who are not averse from eating Redwing eggs and young.

The defense proceeds according to pattern. Initially each bird advertises ownership by displaying visual and vocal signals from the various watchtowers along his borders. If an intruding bird fails to heed the warning, he may be greeted with very insistent scold notes such as defeated the unfortunate Brown Thrasher. When these are ignored, a more aggressive display might be used.

In the animal world each aggressive display reveals the degree of hostility "felt" by an individual. While confronted with a competitor, a bird experiences in varying degrees the conflicting desires to attack and flee. The defendant initially wants to attack and the trespasser to flee. Such black and white encounters generally result in the defendant's flying at the intruder and evicting him by sheer force of motivation.

Among songbirds, if the intruder does not flee when attacked, the two birds are likely to find themselves face to face on a perch. Then the chances are that both birds enter a gray zone where they feel equal desires to attack and flee. The game is on. Each displays until the balance is upset and one—strongly moved to escape—flies away.

When a singing Wood Thrush first sees a competitor in his territory he stops singing, raises his crest, slightly spreads his breast feathers, and emits notes of alarm. If these displays do not drive off the intruder, the defender performs the supplanting flight where he tries to evict the stranger by landing more or less on top of him. Sometimes the intruder remains through this with the result that the flier lands very close to him. At such proximity the defender may perform a shouting spread of the breast feathers which usually causes the departure of the other.

A Gray-cheeked Thrush lands on a perch and is joined by another who lands within a foot of the first. Immediately the first bird pulls himself up as tall as possible. The second does likewise, then both pause. Instantly the first bird flattens into a horizontal stretch and gapes—the bite threat—at the second, who flees, unbitten yet defeated.

This same display may be used in a modified form by an intensely hostile Wood Thrush. When suddenly confronted with an unpleasant situation the body is leveled like a snarling dog, the head feathers compressed with the wish to escape, and the body feathers fluffed in the attitude of attack. The final weapon is the gaping bill, which directs at the enemy the bright yellow mouth lining and is used only when the opponent is within a foot or two of the displaying bird. Unless the opponent can outdisplay the defender in this final parry, he leaves.

When faced with opposition, the Redwing stops singing, ruffles his black and red feathers, and extends his length by pointing his bill upward. If that fails to deter the intruder, the defender flies directly at him, crash-landing with open bill and simultaneously rolling out an avian growl. This usually sends the enemy off, another case of ruffled feathers winning out.

One pair of Redwing males called a draw in their ritual. For a week both had been claiming the same pine tree as their main post, but each had managed to call from it when the other was not there. One evening when the first male was calling from the bottom branch of the tree, the second landed on the opposite side. Then the following game occurred.

The first male, with his black feathers depressed but his epaulettes blazing, pointed his bill straight up and held this position until the other did likewise. Then he relaxed, and a moment later jumped to the next higher branch where he repeated his display. The other male, not to be outdone, jumped up to the same height and also displayed. Then the first bird again went up a rung, the two repeating the process until the very top branch was reached. As the two birds seemed to wonder what would come next, a grackle flew in and the first male gave chase, leaving the second preening on the tree.

Occasionally even these displays do not work. Then the defendant must give chase and perhaps actually fight. Songbirds fly at their opponents with bills snapping and feet forward and spread. When the contenders meet, they lock feet and turn into a few ounces of feathered ferocity. One tangle usually drives the intruder away. If he returns for another, the defendant may sportingly compromise by ceding some land along one edge, so long as the concession does not threaten his own well-being. When there is no room to spare, the chase will continue until the weaker is exhausted.

Such a battle was waged between two Bald Eagles who fell talon-tangled from a high treetop into a palmetto thicket at the base of the tree. After ten minutes of piercing screams, silence fell and one eagle flew out of the thicket looking the worse for wear. The other was not seen to leave.

After mating, territorial defense is naturally extended to include the wife. Although each female assiduously guards her own nest territory within that of the male, she sometimes wanders next door. Ordinarily the defending male chases her home and her own mate pays no attention. But if she draws a sexual display from the stranger, her mate immediately flies to the scene and reclaims the vamp. One way of obtaining recognition!

Most animals are guilty of frequent transgressions over lines that are meant to be observed. Although birds defend their own territories vigorously, most have a tendency to wander. Often they can be seen trespassing far from home, feeding surreptitiously when the owner-bird is either unaware or off trespassing elsewhere. Such behavior suggests that even among birds, fences are useless when the builder is away.

IV Courtship

It is mid-May in the north. The air is soft and the hardwood forests respond to the warm weightless flow of the sun's language. The hushed air pops with the noise of unfolding leaves and lifts the burden of dampness from the filmy new wings of emerging creatures. The forest floor stirs with the mysterious opening of vulnerable flowers, and the mossy cold rocks of mountain streams give birth to iridescent emerald and turquoise damselflies. Alert birds view the dynamic scene from their perches in the sun, while the stillness throbs with the unloosed excitement of those who have yet to create. Spring has burst into bloom.

From the giddy top of a towering spruce trickles a warbling stream of unhurried challenge. Below, the passerby halts to hear the song-ster again. Listen. They come—twenty notes at least pouring out of the tree. Four thousand times a day this song proclaims the presence of the invisible singer to unmated rivals and females close by. He is the pale gray-green Warbling Vireo, feathered like the leaves he sings in—a camouflage for a gifted singer.

Thus the bird world is gradually being caught up in the intensely absorbing business of securing mates through a myriad of courtship displays, all designed to close the gap between the sexes.

The proverbial war between the sexes has been graphically worked out for parrots who pair for life. If "f" symbolizes flee, "a" attack, and "c" copulate, faC represents the happy state for both birds when the planting of the seed takes place.

At the outset of courtship, the male usually experiences a conflict between fleeing from his intended and copulating with her, produc-ing an FaC. At the same time the female feels the single urge to attack, fAc. It is this impossible situation that demands ameliora-tion through courtship, the goal toward which the male functions unto success. For days or perhaps weeks, the male displays before the female, stimulating her to reach the physiological state where she is able to respond to him sexually. Once she attains this period of receptivity, both birds may elicit copulation by short-term displays, seconds or minutes, to one another. The end result is that the male gradually loses his fear and the female her aggressive tendencies, and the ideal faC is reached. The essence of the age-old problem and its solution is typically

$$FaC + fAc \text{ becomes } faC.$$

All courtship displays function toward the successful transfer of the male seed to the female. These displays generally consist of var-ious vocal and visual signals used alone or in combination. Unlike humans who behave as personality and circumstance dictate, birds respond to one another in highly stereotyped fashion to the extent that a particular display must be used by one bird in order to set off the expected response in another. Where certain displays between birds of different species can be understood by all, those connected with reproduction are intraspecific, or generally recognized only by individuals within a species. This aids in the perpetuating of pure-breds. A simple example of a highly ritualized courtship is to be found in the European version of our Laughing Gull, the monogamous Black-headed Gull.

The elegant male first makes known his availability by giving the long call, a drawn-out cry addressed to the sky and any unmated females flying by. A female lands next to the caller. At this her first visit he is not sure of her intentions or readiness to copulate, so undergoes the conflict between fleeing and staying.

Lowering his body into the horizontal characteristic of the hostile display, he points his bill forward and upward (to alleviate the hostility) and by keeping his body parallel to hers, shows only half of his frightening black mask. The friendly female responds by adopting the same posture. The significant point here is that the birds do not face each other, which would be a literal affront.

From this "forward" the male suddenly snaps into the third and final first-date display. Both birds, standing upright and next to each other, turn their heads away and completely conceal their black masks from one another. The hostile nature of this "upright" is softened by the facing away.

After this, the female may fly off to visit several other males. Later she may return for more, thus showing preference for a certain male. Each time she returns, the same ritual is performed, always more gracefully as the pair become used to one another. When they have lost their fear, the male advances into courtship feeding, which announces pair formation and the end of the trials of courtship.

What happens when genetic wires get crossed is less fortunate and paradoxically points up the importance of the appropriate ritual. In Ithaca, New York, a Redhead x Shoveler duck had catastrophic difficulties when it came to courting other ducks. When the other drakes were cruising around the pond courting the hens in the fashion of either diving or dabbling ducks, the hybrid erupted in a strange ritual combining both. The sad result was that the other ducks ignored him because his odd behavior was acceptable to no one.

A similar case involved a Sharp-tailed Grouse x Greater Prairie Chicken hybrid that was capering on the booming grounds of the Greater Prairie Chicken in Wisconsin. In response to his initial booming (prairie chicken!) a rival came over and challenged him to a duel. The unfortunate creature accepted in Sharp-tailed Grouse language which the contender did not recognize. So the purebred called the whole thing off by returning flabbergasted to his own territory.

When cocks begin to challenge for mates, sunrise and sunset the world around are accompanied by purposeful sounds.

In the chilly predawn gray of the Haitian mountain mists, a long minor thrushtone rises out of the dew-covered tree fern stumps, is held with thrilling richness for several seconds, and dies. Seconds later another higher note breaks the intervening silence and flies down the pine-covered mountainside to the valley below. The gentle women padding their barefoot way to market with sugarcane on their heads pause momentarily to hear the minor matins. Thrice more come the strong rich tones from the forest floor—each pure call sustained unto fulfillment. Then the invisible brown Musician Bird falls silent, and the women continue on their way as the first thin sunbeams cut the mist of the waking forest.

Later in the day another songster pipes war and peace over the wildest areas of the United States, claiming them as the sun goes down and frogs tentatively begin their chorus. The Hermit Thrush rings out his opening flutelike tone—subsequent notes fly bell-like up to beyond the range of human hearing, the solo echoing the peace of one soul sharing solitude with another.

These are two of the songbirds, those small perching birds who use their varied musical narratives to simultaneously warn away and woo birds within range of hearing.

There are almost as many types of auditory lures as there are forms of birds. Songbirds have evolved elaborate songs which, in some instances, may compensate for small size or drab coloring. In wild Chaffinches, songs can be learned only during the first thirteen months of the bird's life. A few features of song are learned from the parents while the young are still in the nest. But during the first breeding season they learn the finer aspects through competing with other males. A peak period is reached in the last few weeks when an attentive bird can learn up to six different songs. This period of learning is brought to a sudden halt by internal changes at the end of the first breeding season.

Other birds have also evolved effective sounds of advertisement. Flickers and sapsuckers make themselves known by their early morning drumming—hammering away on dead limbs, transformer boxes, drainpipes, and tin roofs in earshattering efforts to call forth potential mates. The crowing of the pheasant rings over fields as the exotic cock warns other males to keep clear of his harem. Whip-poor-wills whistle their name through the nights of spring and early summer, often from the preferred back porch of an inhabited house.

The Common Nighthawk comes out in late twilight and swoops silently through the darkening sky, marking off the buggy stillness with an emphatic beert uttered every four or five seconds. When he becomes almost invisible in the darkness, he mounts the sky a hundred feet above ground, hovers there, then plunges earthward, coming out of the dive ten feet above ground with a booming *vroom* that can be heard half a mile distant.

Inland lakes hemmed in by walls of rock echo the spectacular courtship calling of the loons. On a peaceful lake a Common Loon suddenly sends up a high musical howl that rings over the water, breaks on the wall, and leaves the mirror trembling in silence. Ten seconds later the bird howls again. Still silence. Three times more. Then a brief answering tremolo from a female floating close by. The male greets her with a quivering call. Then the pair tremolo together, calling with increasing frequency and fervor until both slide up into exultant shrieks of ecstasy. Three-beat cadences of bell-like arpeggios measure off this climactic plateau for a dozen phrases —then a sudden ringing lull settles as the echoes fly away over the water's surface.

Though human experience by and large is more familiar with these and other sounds of courtship, there are many less-known visual aspects ranging from the subtle signals of the monogamous Sparrow Hawk to the elaborate dance spread of the promiscuous argus pheasants. Among the monogamous birds some of these displays are continued throughout the nesting period to maintain the pair bond, which might otherwise suffer when the incubating female loses her receptivity.

Some birds appear to have no courtship displays whatever. But this is a failing of the human eye rather than lack of communication between the birds. When a pair of Sparrow Hawks are together there is no apparent courtship display, but suddenly the relationship may be consummated. Their signals are too subtle for even a trained eye to discern.

Most of the small birds combine mothlike flights with plumage displays and sounds. The Pin-tailed Widow Bird hovers over the female, jerking the four long tail feathers up and down with each wingbeat so they cascade down over the enchanted hen. The Black-faced Grassquit performs a slow arching flight where the male comes to perch near the female. There with buzzing voice he vibrates his spread wings, the whole set off by the spread tail. The kinglets,

American Ovenbirds, and kingbirds erect the brilliant red, yellow, or orange crests that transform their usually drab heads into captivating jewels.

The Ruffed Grouse calls the female to his log by drumming the air with his stiffened wings. Starting with a resounding single boom per second the tempo increases rapidly to a continuous boom when the wings beat faster than the eye can see. As the hen appears, the male becomes a different bird, displaying like the well-known Thanksgiving turkey. The black and white striped tail is elevated and spread to form a magnificent fan. The wingtips are lowered to the feet, and the black collar is erected to form an immense ruff around the head. The bird struts with charming dignity up and down the drumming log, convulsively pulling his neck in and out so that the collar is in constant motion, the whole accompanied by deep soft booming sounds.

In Australia and New Guinea live a group of drab birds who compensate for their lack of color by using ingenuity. These are the bowerbirds whose name derives from their elaborate courtship bowers. The most highly colored of these birds clear simple areas on the ground. The dullest members construct highly elaborate stick walls to contain a breezeway and decorate them with colored objects or even "paint" made of berries. Whatever type of bower is built, it serves as the center of the male's territory where he courts and couples.

On the grasslands of New Guinea, Lauterbach's Bowerbird rearranges some of the thousand ornaments that decorate his bower, and pokes reinforcing sticks into the walls. The bower consists of two main walls a foot high, formed by vertically placed sticks, and the nuptial chamber between. Opposite each end of the breezeway is another wall which shuts off the chamber from public view. On the floor of the bower is a carefully assembled collection of grayish stones and colored berries. Spilling out both ends are the rest of the ornaments—large red, blue, and green berries. These spheres are the drab bird's saving grace.

Over several weeks the busy male stops every few minutes to call a potential mate. One day a female who has come several times before, then departed, appears near the bower. She looks exactly like the male. Quickly he picks up a large red berry in his bill, and with great concentration starts his insinuating dance at the opposite end of the bower. The ready female watches down the alley that separates them. As the minutes pass, she is lured hop by hop into the nuptial chamber. When she reaches the middle and flattens herself on the grass floor, the cock flies onto her back and proves the value of seduction by material means.

For monogamous birds, bowerbirds lead a solitary existence. The male tends his bower for weeks before the female finally comes around to copulating. Afterward, she goes off into the surrounding jungle, builds a nest, and raises the family while her mate continues to keep bower and defend his property. When the young have fledged, the female rejoins her mate with the brood and they flock with other families for the winter.

A small proportion of birds are polygamous, having several mates at the same time. Among them are various members of the oriole and blackbird family. Fortunately the hens are in different stages of the reproductive cycle so that males are not burdened with the task of winning two females at the same time.

The courtship display of the Redwing is usually a mutual affair, although by virtue of his plumage the male is the more appealing to the human eye. When a female enters a territory the male gives the song spread where he sings and ruffles his feathers simultaneously. As the female becomes interested, both birds indulge repeatedly in the spread while clinging to their swaying reeds. As the most intense period of courtship is reached, the male's erected epaulettes are vibrated during the spread. The significance of the erected red feathers can be appreciated by the fact that they are concealed when the male is feeding or trespassing and when a hawk appears overhead, all instances when he is subject to danger.

Courtship displays in the promiscuous birds—those who copulate indiscriminately and casually—are probably more spectacular than those of any other group. As a rule promiscuous birds are endowed with unusually striking feather forms, booming sacs, or other features that become exaggerated as the degree of promiscuity increases—a male who copulates with a dozen hens passes on twelve times as many genetic characters as he who joins with one. The main difference between the promiscuous male and the polygamous is that the former defends none of his "mates."

One of the most promiscuous of American birds is the Ruby-throated Hummingbird. Diminutive in size, it is gay in every sense of the word. In courtship, the female perches on a low twig. Then the male performs a U-shaped dive, swooping up before the feminine bill and displaying from every angle his iridescent feathers. A spectacular change occurs when the black throat is suddenly transformed into a dazzling ruby gorget.

Other such Americans are the declining prairie chickens. At the beginning and end of each day, ten to forty brownish cocks gather at a display area to challenge one another for the domination of the females who are expected. Like a mechanical toy, each cock drops his stiffened wings, lowers his head, and runs forward a few steps. He stops and inflates to bursting a pair of orange air sacs on the sides of his neck which suddenly deflate with a resounding boom. Then he scuttles on and booms again. The females gather casually as the booms increase, and gradually each approaches one of the few dominant cocks.

With a hen in attendance, the male stops the dance and stands before her. He fluffs out all his feathers, raises his black-rimmed ear tufts and tail, and spreads his wingtips to the ground. After several moments the hen may signal that she is ready, the moment is shared, and she scurries off to build her nest.

In the forests of South America live the Yellow-thighed Manakins, small birds who stage communal courtship dances surpassed only by some birds of paradise. Several of these black-red-yellow birds convene in an area large enough for each male to have his own display limb. A female is attracted by calls or dance noises, and all the males compete for her attention. She shows her preference for one who then begins his display.

Pulling himself up as tall as he can, he exposes the bright yellow thighs that are to be the center of his dance. Suddenly he reverses his position on the limb, then turns back again, repeating the turns in such rapid sequence that a whirring color wheel is created. The peripheral red head whirls around the jet black body and the yellow hub. Having impressed the female, he may move closer to face her. Snapping his wings and buzzing continuously he jiggles backward for one foot, returns, and repeats the performance. The female is unable to resist.

Among manakins the courtship instinct is so strong that in the absence of a female the males are likely to display to each other. Some pairs of males spend much time together, possibly missing opportunities to win females.

Probably the most fantastic birds in the world are the birds of paradise found in Australia and New Guinea. These have the most elaborate courtship plumes of any birds alive. They include capes, tails, wires, and whips, all of which spring to life when the bird is displaying. It is thought that the elaborate plumes help prevent the females from choosing the wrong bird in the hasty meeting-and-mating pattern of the family.

The seven-inch Magnificent Bird of Paradise wears a bright yellow collar over a deep red back and shiny green front. Springing out from the center of the tail are two sickle-shaped feathers. Other than these the bird has no plumes, but is very resourceful. Like the gardening bowerbirds, this bird clears an area of the forest floor around the base of a young tree. Then he removes some of the overhead leaves to let the skylight through to his dance stage. So illumined he calls and a female enters. First he dances on the ground, then walks up the side of the tree. The high point is reached when the elevated bird leans backward into space and directs his shining green and gold plumage to the lightshaft, thus becoming a dazzling light before the eyes of his marveling visitor.

In Malaya lives another bird who is so resplendent that a mere posture is cause enough for females to yield. In the late afternoon the last rays of sun filter through the jungle canopy and fall on an immaculate clearing of ground surrounded by ancient trees. This is the age-old dance arena of an argus pheasant.

Entering the stage by a trodden path from out of the underbrush, the bird walks tentatively into the spotlight and calls into the jungle. There is no answer. A few minutes later he calls again. Still no answer. He sees a twig that has fallen onto the stage, picks it up and discards it at the forest edge. Again his voice rings. From far away comes the reply of a hen. After several more exchanges she finally arrives at the edge of the clearing and takes her place in the shadows.

The cock responds. Slowly he erects the four-foot-long tail and the wing plumes, bringing them up and forward over his head and back, which are lost behind the resultant fan. Along the veins of the feathers are huge "eyes" of subtle color. Every few seconds the bird begins to quiver—the eyes are set in motion so the fan becomes a shimmering wheel of shadows and lights. The display lasts for several minutes, during which the curious cock may poke his head out to see how the hen is reacting. During previous visits she has disappeared back into the jungle when he was not looking. This time she has advanced onto the stage, where she silently submits to him.

Thus promiscuous cocks call, court, and copulate in one package deal, and their momentary joys disappear into the forest to fend for themselves.

Courtship brings together two individuals to form a pair and raise a family. This mutual agreement to pair off is known as mating, a relationship which is unknown to promiscuous species.

Although some birds such as ducks and seabirds mate while they are still in their winter flocks, the vast majority mate as a logical step in the spring courtship.

Among birds where the sexes are dressed alike, courtship and mating are confusing at first. Given no clues in dress, the males distinguish the interested females from rival males and transient females by their responsive postures. Such a problem arose with two British Robins who were living bachelor lives in adjoining territories. One day, as spots of sunlight flew across her sodden feeding ground, the maiden Robin felt it was time to wander next door. Slowly she walked and fed her way into the territory of the bachelor. Seeing the trespasser, the cock flew at her and displayed his breast to show that he owned that land. The visitor held her ground. Instead of displaying as a rival or retreating as a transient, she uttered a note and flew right up to the cock. He repeated his threat and she moved even closer. The two birds became very excited by their new experience and continued the sallies for two days until they formed a pair.

Following mating, the two were slow in adjusting to one another. Sometimes one would approach the other and be met with a threat. As always where hostility wanes, their behavior mellowed with time and they became as one. The threats and singing eventually stopped, signifying that all was proceeding according to Hoyle. (Males often cease singing once they have mated, only to resume a few days later when the female becomes receptive.)

Captive parrots form pairs in a matter of hours. Members of a flock interrelate by mutual preening and other activities. Through such close contact certain birds come to feel in harmony with others. Within a few hours pairs who prefer one another's company to that of the group may be seen engaged in courtship feeding, apparently having formed a lifetime partnership.

Courtship feeding often serves as a pair bond throughout the relationship. It is one of the ways by which birds can maintain a certain intimacy during and after the period of receptivity and bears little relation to the need for food. Witness the captive Robin who stood for minutes up to her knees in worms, gaping and waiting for her obtuse and inexperienced mate to feed her.

Under certain conditions pair formation can result in homosexual relationships. Young captive parrots of the species where the sexes look alike sometimes form homosexual pairs which break up as the members mature. Adults normally are heterosexual, but birds deprived of potential mates of the opposite sex readily form homosexual pairs where one assumes the male role and the other the female. The physiological impact of such relationships can be seen in female pairs where both build the nest, lay their eggs, and incubate simultaneously. Alas, the setup lacks only a handful of sperms.

The usual marriage relationship is monogamy. But the duration of the bond varies from a lifetime among the faithful swans to a single brood in House Wrens.

Ravens, parrots, eagles, geese, and swans are the birds who most consistently renew their bonds of devotion and spend their lives together. In the wild this could mean ten years more or less, in captivity it could last over thirty.

There are numerous stories telling of the death of one of a pair and the inability of the survivor to remate, or even live on. Where swans are said to be perfect examples of fidelity, geese seem to vary. One rare instance is cited where a fox killed a Canada Goose and the mate passed away the following day. But other geese have shattered the fidelity image by divorcing and remating with someone else.

Actually swans and geese have both been known to indulge in extramarital meanderings. When a male is defending his nest territory from all intruders he is harshly opposed to the advances of the most attractive unmated females. But should he meet such a solicitor across the pond while off duty, he is very likely to serve her, as he is less preoccupied with defense.

Most birds lack the attachment necessary for lifetime relationships and mate for several years or less. Gulls and terns, penguins, chickadees, crows, and jays remate year after year, possibly keeping their bonds through the winter. Ducks and songbirds are believed to mate for one season only. Remating may be happenstance resulting from the instinct to return to the old nesting area.

The Wood Duck is adjustable in this respect. The drake forsakes his old territory and follows each new mate back to her old nesting area, going one year to Maine and the next to California. House Wrens, bluebirds, and other hole-nesters commonly change mates between broods of one summer.

The Brewer's Blackbird follows no set marriage pattern and is remarkably realistic and pragmatic in his affairs. Normally when the number of females equals the number of males, monogamous pairings result. But when the females outnumber the males two to one, the males take on several wives, a practice recognized by some cultured human societies, tending year after year to retain the favored mate of the preceding year.

Polygamy is practiced around the world. Here in the United States, Redwings, meadowlarks, Yellow-headed Blackbirds, and Ring-necked Pheasants aid and covet more than one wife. In the Old World, female Winter Wrens share a husband. The Asiatic weavers indulge in progressive polygamy whereby the male builds a nest, settles a mate into it, and starts building another. In the course of three months he will have a small trio of wives each in a different stage of nesting. In fact, incidents of polygamy can be found in nearly every kind of bird at one time or another.

For every Redwing who has one wife, there are probably four who have two or more. Pair formation is quick. If a female visits a territory, finds a suitable nest site, and lingers long enough to stimulate the male, he feels that she is his and the pair is formed. There may follow a period of three weeks until the eggs are laid, during which the bond is crystallized by a variety of displays.

One is the symbolic selection of a nest site by the male. Ahead of the female he crawls liquidly through the cattail jungle with his black wings held over his back. As he goes, he simulates nest-building by actually biting off bits of reed and manipulating them with his bill. All of this suggestive action is to activate the female's interest in the more laborious aspects of nesting.

Another display used on and off with the above is the chase. The male suddenly dives off his perch at the female, who takes off. If he catches her he usually gives a series of strong pecks to her rump and holds on as they tumble through the air, then speed back to the territory.

Once the female reaches the receptive stage, instead of fleeing from the male and leading a chase she crouches in the invitatory display. With bill and tail pointed skyward she flutters her wings and whimpers, helpless as she is. Like a stiff-legged windup toy the male approaches her with outspread wings vibrating, bill and tail down, feathers fluffed out, and mounts her from behind. Copulation lasts two or three seconds. Sometimes the female solicits attention and the male ignores her completely—the timing is very important.

Although the male soon turns his interest to acquiring another mate, this pair call one another until the mother takes her fledglings from the territory. The chances are she will return the following year.

There is one breed of Redwing which is avoided by mated females and their young—the first-year male. Females dive into the cattails whenever they see such a bird approaching, and their mates fly to their aid in response to the cries. The young are no more kind in responding to his advances with the repelling bill-tilting posture. First-year males sometimes mount young birds, mistaking their food-begging for invitatory display with which they have so far had little experience. This is easily done as the difference between the two is so slight as to be almost a matter of outlook. In that respect the two are worlds apart.

The acquisition of several husbands by one energetic female is

also a cosmopolitan practice. Tinamous, bustards, Old World cuckoos, and phalaropes may have several husbands.

There seems to be some variation among the phalaropes as to how much care the female gives her young. In the Red Phalarope the male does most of the work from nest-building on. Some people have observed the female remaining near the nest during a large part of the parental care period. Others note that she is conspicuous by her absence. Where the Wilson's female sometimes has two mates and may even raise two families, the female Northern is thought to be monogamous. Her mate is typical of many birds in that he becomes promiscuous and is easily seduced by any female, but it is probable that he succeeds only with his own mate. As he nears the nest-building phase of his cycle he joins his mate in the nest-scraping ceremony, which stimulates her to choose a nest site and him to build. The pair stay close together until incubation is well under way. Then she usually leaves and may go offshore to join other females. It seems to be universally true that some females make better husbands and some males better wives.

One unusual case among longspurs occurred when the males outnumbered the females. Three cocks were found tending one hen on her nest, a sensible and happy adjustment to an unfortunate situation. Usually extra males form a bachelor population. Probably these three were driven to unusual behavior by hormones, which account for many aberrations, or two had somehow lost their mates.

Promiscuity is unusual for most birds, common for others. Old World cuckoos are parasitic species who often copulate with acceptable acquaintances met while hunting for a foster nest. Flocks of Boat-tailed Grackle males wander over the Florida flats mounting the females who come to greet them, much like sailors passing through ports. The birds of paradise and some grouse need no further mention as being consistently promiscuous and fascinating. One Sage Grouse resplendent in his oversize white vest and pinnated tail mounted twenty-one hens in one morning.

The European Oystercatcher plays the field during courtship, promiscuously copulating with a variety of hens. When the right one comes along, however, the cock takes her as his mate and the pair settle into a monogamous nesting relationship—a practice that has become popular in most human societies.

Avian coupling is ordinarily undertaken in privacy, but it is often accompanied by an outpouring of squealings that readily betray what is happening and where.

For instance, a sleep-shattering kee-yer kee-yer kee-yer bursts suddenly into the early morning stillness and shoots down to earth from the giddy heights of an Australian pine. On a branch stands the buffy Red-shouldered Hawk, tail up and head stretched forward, screaming for her mate across acres of palmetto. From far away comes his reply. Then in enthusiastic exchange of love greetings the air is rent with their passionate cries. Skimming over the tops of the trees the smaller hawk appears. With wings flapping strongly he swoops up onto the branch next to his mate. With her scream eliding into a squeal she flattens her body against the solid branch and looks at her mate. He spreads his broad wings and lifting himself up he drops onto her back. As he gracefully holds his balance with the thrashing wings, their open beaks let out mewing cries that ascend quickly to a straining pitch until there is no further need, and her mate dismounts to sit quietly beside her. She looks soft, peaceful, and vulnerable—he looks bewildered. After a minute or two his hunting instinct returns and he flies off, leaving her alone on the branch watching him disappear behind the treetops from whence he had come.

These hawks will copulate several times a day as they build their bulky nest during the weeks prior to incubation and the onset of parental duties. Other birds, such as owls and ducks, start months before nesting. But most females are receptive for a precious few days between nest-building and incubation, which helps assure the fertilization of the eggs. During this time, males generally do their most intensive displaying in response to their highly receptive mates.

A pair of English Sparrows made hay while the sun was shining by copulating fourteen times in succession, taking five seconds on and five off. When the male was spent the female was still fluttering her wings and calling for more.

Among parrots copulation is frequent and may last for five or six minutes. Rather than being a cut-and-dried biological event it seems to be an enjoyable way of maintaining the pair bond. This instrumental aspect of copulation is borne out by the fact that females often mount the males. The birds are bent on stimulating one another without regard to form.

The chances of mutual enjoyment are greatly increased by a certain pattern of preliminary behavior which is followed by experienced individuals, generally the older birds. When the hen is ready to receive the cock, she lowers her head, humps her back, and gives a note of invitation or some other signal. Inexperienced males sometimes need further clues but the worldly cock immediately mounts his joy. The resulting posture can be held for seconds or minutes, and can be achieved in the air, on land, on water, or even underwater by the birds at home in each medium.

An interesting aspect of copulation in parrots who look alike is the male's need for the female to maintain visible signs characteristic of her sex. During copulation the female ruffles her wrists and tilts her head to show her surmounted partner the ruffled cheeks and throat. If for some reason she lapses out of this feminine ruffle the male dismounts and resumes his arousal displays.

Unless the cock is far ahead of the hen in the cycle, he is likely to wait for her invitation. If he jumps her she is apt to look indifferent and bored and nothing of biological importance is accomplished.

One pair of crimson-billed Laughing Gulls underwent an experience together where neither one was responding favorably to the other. Without any signal from the hen, the cock flew up onto her back. There with wings tentatively but constantly beating he stood undecided about what to do next. The hen took a few heavy steps and he rode along looking down at her questioningly, unable to tell why she was walking. She looked up at him to discern why he was standing on her back.

After two or three repeats the cock thought that if he switched ends his problem might be solved. He turned around on her back as does a tightrope walker so his head was over her tail, and still things did not seem right. Reversing his position again he tried to copulate with his beloved, but she started walking again. So defeated, he dismounted and stood next to her, who looked at him as if to say "nice to have your feet on the ground again."

A ready hen on the other hand can be oblivious as to who is above her. A captive cock mounted a captive hen only to be pushed off by another cock who hopped on to complete the act. A wild Redwing hen likewise received two males in the space of a moment. Neither captive nor wild hen was at all perturbed by the switch in mates.

The physiology of avian copulation is simpler than that of the mammals, and probably less efficient. Except for ducks who generally mate underwater, geese, ostriches, and tinamous, birds have no intromittent organ. Beneath the tail is a vestibular opening called the cloaca which functions both as an outlet for waste and a pas-

sageway for the sex cells. When the cock mounts the hen he presses his cloaca to hers, and with the help of muscular contractions transfers nearly two billion sperm which pass with luck directly into the hen. Parrots who have successfully received such gifts have reddened and swollen cloacas where those who have not been so fertilized remain small and dry.

Although some foresighted females will not allow their mates to mount them until the nest is nearly complete, most couples build and mate alternately. Usually the female is receptive until the eggs are laid; then her mating urge is displaced by the incubative. In the interim she usually prepares for the inevitable appearance of fertile eggs by building some sort of nest.

VI Nest Building

For a number of weeks the air has been full of the anvil ring of Cardinals, the mewing of Brown Thrashers, the scolding clucks of Mockingbirds, the chucking of the Pileated Woodpecker, the frog-like loud chirring of the Red-bellied Woodpecker, and the secretive song of the White-eyed Vireo. Suddenly one day the usual sounds seem muffled under a blanket of busy silence.

Outside in the Australian pine, two Red-bellies churr softly to one another. In the sun-roasted corner of the yard the White-eyed Vireo repeats chip-cheerio-wee-chick from the shiny leather-leaved sea grape. In the strangler fig a Pileated Woodpecker, with his bushy red crest erected, strips small branches of their succulent berries while a frantic Mockingbird flies at him again and again in defense of his precious food supply.

Close to the house the stubby remains of a lime tree, torn apart by a hurricane, is alive with quick movements. There are numerous strands of dead grass two or three feet in length trailing out from the center of the tree. Every few seconds one is jerked a few inches shorter. Within the darkness is the busy silhouette of a bird twisting about in one spot, yanking in the grasses and shaping them into a nest lining. Five yards away in the neighboring tree stands her apparent mate, a vibrant red Cardinal perching black-faced in the shade of a branch, upright and attentive, guarding his territory with aplomb. Not a sound passes between them. There is silent understanding—the male guards his mate while she builds the nest.

Nesting normally follows courting and mating. But most birds can nest only in the presence of visual releasers which they associate with nesting. The need for specific conditions has resulted in several distinct races of Canada Geese and swans who return year after year to the same locale, inbreeding all the while. Ducks are much more cosmopolitan, the undemanding males having produced numerous hybrids the world over. The females on the other hand are very attached to the habitat where they were born. This explains why a drake who meets a hen on the wintering grounds nearly always returns to her home to breed. Generally, wild ducks moved to a pond will court and mate at the new home. But the unhappy female cannot continue on to lay eggs unless the right releasers are present. The necessity of outside releasers may be a way of assuring constant nesting populations in suitable locales from year to year. This attachment to the place of birth makes it difficult if not impossible for birds to find new nesting places when the old are wiped out.

Birds can be found nesting on land anywhere in the world. One can nest in the desert while another can nest in the Arctic. One will nest underground while another will use a treetop. Nearly every natural niche can attract some kind of bird.

A nest is primarily a protective housing for the delicate eggs to be placed in. Some nests, such as those of geese, will be deserted after the eggs hatch, and are not very elaborate. Others like those made by Redwings will shelter the young until they are ready to leave the nest. These are more stable affairs.

Many birds make no nest at all. The most daring of these are the fairy terns of the South Pacific islands who lay their single egg on the horizontal branch of a tree, using neither glue nor concavity to help it stay put. Murres are cliff-dwelling seabirds who lay their single egg on the bare rock high above the sea, usually on a ledge just wide enough to hold the nesting bird.

Most birds must make an effort to keep their eggs at home. The few shorebirds who nest on beaches scoop a depression in the sand to keep their four eggs together. The Nighthawk lays her two eggs on gravel. The Whip-poor-will lays its two eggs on a few leaves pulled together. The jaçana drops her four eggs on a floating lily pad lavishly topped with hollow stems. The Emperor Penguin pulls its single egg up on the feet as soon as it is laid, tucks it under the tummy flap, and should not walk.

Other birds build crude nests on the ground. Gulls and terns often nest in colonies, laying their eggs on a mat of grass stems. Ducks, geese, and swans all build substantial nests in a depression on the ground and line them with small sticks, grasses, and their own down. The eiders' down is so abundant that the female covers her eggs with a blanket when she leaves them. The Canada Goose rarely departs from the usual ground nest and takes over an old hawk nest high up in a tree.

The Wood Duck and Goldeneye nest in tree holes. The grebes build their floating nests loosely anchored to vegetation—the hollow stems allow the nest to rise and fall with the water level.

Meadowlarks and Ovenbirds build roofs over a concavity in the ground, the former building a grass dome and the latter a dome of leaves from her woodland home.

A few birds nest beneath the surface of the ground. Burrowing Owls excavate a burrow five to ten feet long at the end of which they place their nest lined with manure, grass, and rootlets. In the West they sometimes use vacated prairie dog burrows, and are in turn displaced by rattlesnakes. Bank Swallows nest in colonies. Each digs a three-foot tunnel straight back into the dirt bank, makes a loose grass cup, and lines it with feathers. Kingfishers excavate tunnels four or five feet back into a bank, delving ahead with their bills and kicking the dirt out behind them.

Above ground can be found a variety of nests ranging from the crude to the highly specialized. The Mourning Dove and New World cuckoos construct flat, drafty nests on tree branches that serve only to support their contents, which can be seen from beneath. The Catbird and Cardinal build crude bowl-shaped nests of twigs and line them with grasses and rootlets.

Crows, hawks, and herons use sticks to build substantial but crude platform nests high in trees, any of which can be used by any of the others, as well as large owls. The Bald Eagle builds a tremendous bowl of sticks and branches which is lined with vast amounts of trash, including tablecloths and broomsticks. Every year something is added as long as the pair survive.

One thirty-five-year-old nest weighed two tons when the aged nest tree finally crashed to the ground. But the eagles using it were not thirty-five years old. Eagles mate for life. When one of the pair dies the other brings a new mate back to the old nest, so nests can far outlast their inmates. One pair built their nest completely around the tree trunk, thereby providing shade throughout the day for the eaglets, who moved around it.

Birds who live in tree nest holes are particularly interesting because of their interdependence. The excavators are the woodpeckers and nuthatches, who are equipped to dig their own holes. When they have moved out, other hole-nesters, such as bluebirds, chickadees, Tree Swallows, and small owls move in. The woodpeckers usually dig their holes a foot deep and the chips form the only nesting material. The same chips can later be used by the owls. Bluebirds build a loose cup of grass and stems at the cavity bottom. The Tree Swallow lines the hole with grasses and makes a little cup of feathers. Chickadees, all of whom excavate their own homes if rotten stumps are available, fill the cavity with mosses and plant down and lay their eggs in a fur-and-feather lining.

Marsh dwellers construct their nests of available reeds and muck for the same reason that tree dwellers use sticks and rootlets—availability. The Redwing builds her first reed nest in five to six days, taking three days for the outside and another three for the interior.

Those individuals whose nests are destroyed make up for lost time by building subsequent ones in three to five days. The reedy basket has its loopholes filled with peat, mud, and bits of moldy wood, and the whole is lined with fine grasses and rushes. Nests made in May are usually short-lived. Then the nest is fastened by milkweed fiber to both dead and living cattail stubs. At the rate of an inch a day the green shoots up so that during the week the open nest is gradually tipped up on its side and the eggs deposited one by one into the lake. By June the vegetation is so high that new nests remain level.

Redwing nests are capable of holding four pounds before they start slipping down their reeds. In spite of their strength and beauty, no nest is ever used twice, the bird building a second nest near the first for her next brood.

Marsh wrens build similar baskets that have the advantage of being closed over with only a side entrance. This small hole decreases the likelihood of eggs falling out. While the females are busy lining the real nest with feathers and fur, the male is busy constructing five or six distracting dummy nests.

Though the songbirds are best known for their voices they are also skilled nest-builders. Robins and Barn Swallows build cementlike structures out of mud and clay. More than most birds, they are dependent on the weather, for during very wet years Robins are often delayed several weeks waiting for puddles to dehydrate into mud. If they make their own mud, a downpour is bound to wash it away unless it is sheltered by a roof. Barn Swallows must nest near clay with which they cement the grasses together. Their nests are lined with chicken feathers, which sometimes causes them to go far. One pair was seen diving into the nest of a Cooper's Hawk where they were retrieving the feathers of a dead chicken that had been left there. This suicidal solution shows the intense need for such feathers, as well as the emergence of the nesting instinct over that of survival.

The Solitary Sandpiper is a shorebird who habitually nests in the woods bordering on northern bogs. Though it prefers the vacated nests of Robins and Rusty Blackbirds, its eggs have also been found in the nests of Cedar Waxwings, Gray Jays, kingbirds, grackles, and the Brewer's Blackbird. The bird can adapt itself to any suitable nest between four and forty feet above ground and never seems to add new nest material to the used.

A sort of bastard nest resulted from the cooperative efforts of two practical female songbirds. A Robin began building her nest in a cedar tree. Before it was finished, a Cardinal took up building on the limb below. In the early stages of construction her nest was destroyed, so she moved up and helped the Robin finish hers. Incubation duties were alternately shared by the hens while the attendant cocks guarded their nest together. Each hen hatched one egg and the young were fed by the method usual for the species, the Robin feeding her nestling worms and the Cardinal delivering her food by regurgitation.

The Chipping Sparrow represents numerous birds who switched from rootlets to horsehair nest linings when horses plowed out the forests of early America. Now that the horse is suffering a marked decline and woods have again grown up, the chippy has returned to her root-gathering.

Goldfinches and Yellow Warblers build very soft-looking nests of grasses and stems into which they incorporate copious amounts of cotton, plant down, and feathers. The nests are generally held together with fibers from dead milkweed stalks. The goldfinch nest is waterproof to the extent that it can hold water for twenty-four hours, an asset that can be fatal to the young of parents who forget to go home in a rainstorm. Both these nests are coveted by deer mice as warm hideouts in which to raise their families during the winter.

Hummingbirds, the Blue-gray Gnatcatcher, and the Eastern Wood Pewee all use lichen and bud scales to camouflage their beautiful and delicate domiciles. The fine nests of the Ruby-throated Hummingbird and Blue-gray Gnatcatcher are held together by spider silk. The Wood Pewee uses bark fibers for the same purpose. All are lined with plant down and appear as lichen-covered knots on the branches where they sit. The Ruby-throat's nest is an exquisite one-ounce bump.

In Malaya and Australia, the crested tree swifts glue minute pieces of bark together to fashion a tiny cup which is attached to the side of a small branch. One egg is laid and cemented to the bottom. The nest is so fragile that the incubating parent must sit across the limb with her feet on the nest rim and the breast feathers fluffed out over the egg.

One of the Indo-Australian swiftlets can make its nest solely with its own saliva. She presses her open mouth against the wall to form an anchor-hold and then proceeds with the rest. Such nests are chiefly valued for bird's nest soup. The Chimney Swift glues twigs to the wall, making a nest so small that when the female incubates, her head and neck appear to be climbing up the wall.

The orioles and weaver finches build the most exaggerated of the pensile nests. The Baltimore Oriole's nest, often seen suspended from limbs over highways, are masterpieces of weaving. They are made of light gray plant fibers, bark, paper, and other materials. The top is bottleneck narrow as a precaution against predators, but the bulbous bottom is swollen to ample size for the active young.

The most obvious hanging nests in the world are those of the prolific and highly destructive Red-billed Weaver of Africa. These relatives of the English Sparrow build colonial nests by the millions. An area of three thousand acres may contain ten million nests which fill the crown of every available tree. Some large trees have been found laden down with five thousand of the masterfully woven globes.

The mass nesting is signaled by the onset of long rainstorms when the birds go to nest as readily as city shoppers dive inside sheltering doorways. The monogamous male builds the gourdlike nest as a courtship gesture. When a female accepts it, the male considers himself paired and copulates with her. Like clockwork she lays the first egg the following day.

Where colonial nesters find themselves living in close proximity, but apart, the communal nesters share a house where all the rooms connect. Such nesters are the starling-size Palm Chats of Haïti and the Sociable Weaverbird of southern Africa.

The Palm Chats build immense globular structures of straws and twigs which sometimes reach ten feet in height and six feet in diameter. These apartment houses are built just beneath the palm crown and shelter up to fifty pairs of birds. Each pair builds a bark-lined mat nest with its own exit to the outside as well as those into the connecting passageways. A Sparrow Hawk often nests within these haystacks without causing much consternation among his fellows. Every twenty minutes or so the apartment will explode from within, the birds bursting out for no apparent reason. The hawk invariably stays at his door to watch the others go out.

The Sociable Weaverbird also builds a large, well-sculptured house of strawlike grasses, the pairs sharing the labor of building the dome roof and the vertical tunnels that lead to the nest chambers just beneath the roof.

There is no hard-and-fast rule dictating that females will build the nests while males gather the food. Birds vary in their domestic behavior almost as much as anyone else. Most monogamous weaverbirds share all aspects of parental care. In the polygamous species the male builds most of the nest and the female cares for the young, leaving the male free to court others. The hole-digging birds usually split the labor efforts. Many of the shorebird males have a penchant for building the "nest," which is rarely needed, and caring for the young.

Most birds arrange their lives so that the male outdoes himself in courtship, when he generally loses weight, and the female does the rest. As she builds the nest he accompanies her everywhere and shows real interest, occasionally trying to help. His primary role as soul mate and protector must suffice as support.

Once her nest is nearly complete, a songbird hen will turn her attention to receiving the cock, whose real function is to put life in the nest.

VII Fertilization

Occasionally an egg gatherer makes a mistake so that the egg containing an embryo ends up at the breakfast table rather than hatching in the nest. Such accidents are costly and infrequent, so most of the eggs we eat are infertile or have been snatched out from under the hen before they had time to grow. The differences between fertile and infertile eggs are slight at their beginnings because both originate the same way.

On the left side of the hen near the backbone lies a gland similar to a bunch of grapes called the ovary. While the hen is in the receptive condition, the ovary produces unfertilized eggs, releasing one "grape" each day into a floating funnel-shaped membrane. This is the free end of the oviduct, the elasticized egg-making tube that arises from the cloaca. The egg, which is a cell nucleus surrounded by yolk, remains in the funnel for nearly twenty minutes, during which time it can be fertilized by a sperm.

Shortly after copulation, the sperm pass from the cloacal cavity through a very small opening into the oviduct. From this entrance they make their way up the twisting, fissured, undulating tube to the top, aided both by the lashing of their long tails and the upward contractions of the oviduct walls. Millions die en route.

The strongest sperm meets the egg at the oviduct's top. On contact the sperm is engulfed by the yolk and drops its tail outside, signaling to the losers that he has won the race for survival. The nuclei of the two cells, each containing half the requirements for life, combine their heritable traits and create a new individual.

Alone, a sex cell is unable to support life and dies. But the two halves together make a whole.

Scientists use astronomical symbols to signify the two sexes. ♂ is the symbol for Mars, the active and masculine planet, and is used to denote the male. ♀ stands for Venus, the gentle and feminine planet, and always means female. Using these it is possible to draw a fertilization equation:

$$♂ = O$$
$$♀ = \text{one boiled egg}$$
$$♂ + ♀ = ☿, \text{ or Life.}$$

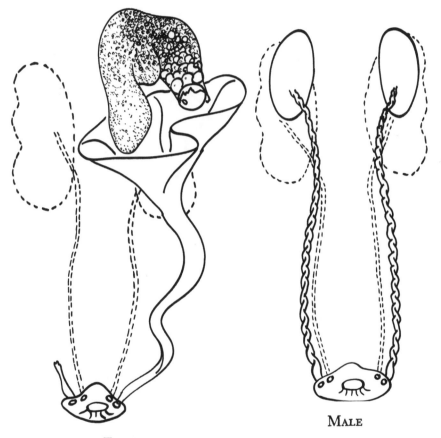

FEMALE

MALE

VIII   The Egg

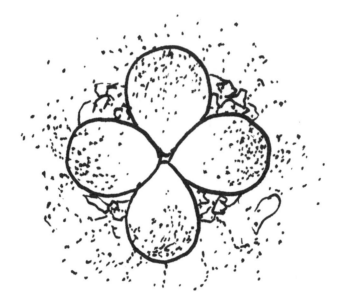

A grebe finished her floating nest one day and the following morning was found dead, her limp body lying across the nest and her sleek black head hanging down to the surface of the water. She died trying to lay an egg which was clogging her oviduct, a victim of nature's scheme for erasing those unfit to perpetuate their kind.

The egg is twenty-four hours in the making after it leaves the ovary. Following fertilization the yolk begins its descent to the cloaca. For three hours it passes by glands that coat it with albumin, or egg white. The yolk is then protected against future shocks by the albumin cushion. For the next hour and a quarter this mass travels past the membrane glands where it is neatly encased in the two membranes that line the shell of a hard-boiled egg. Finally the shapeless egg enters the shell gland through which it moves in eighteen hours, receiving liquid shell and the color pigments. The shell hardens as the egg passes, large end first, to the outside through the vagina and cloaca.

The egg is a classic example of simple and functional modern design dating from dinosaur days. The new life is supplied with yolk and albumin as food, and the albumin shields it from the shocks it will receive. The embryo will always rest on top of the yolk nearest the heat of the incubator because the heavy yolk pivots ingeniously on the ropelike chalaza present at both ends. An air sac at the large end will allow the bird to breathe while it is hatching but still within the egg. The whole is protected by a remarkably firm shell possessed with the strength of the cylinder. Given a lawn to land on, the egg can be thrown over a house and picked up unbroken.

The egg is a living organism. Because the shell allows oxygen to enter the interior and gaseous wastes to filter out, it can be said to breathe. A hot egg sweats—a completely submerged egg drowns.

The seat of life can be seen as a white spot resting on the top of the yolk. Around the spot is an area of yellow lighter than the main yolk. This is the germinal disc of living cells. When sufficient heat is applied, the edges of this disc will spread out, down, and around the yolk until they converge at the bottom. The yolk will then be enclosed by cells destined to specialize as blood, nerve, muscle, skin, bone, and the other types of cells. In the interim the cell sac will draw food from the yolk and deliver it, via a simple circulatory system, to the embryo resting on top.

When the egg leaves the warmth of the oviduct and is popped into the cold world, cell development is arrested until incubation begins.

The capacity of one ostrich egg would equal that of twenty-five chicken eggs or five thousand hummingbird eggs. One chicken egg would hold the contents of two hundred hummingbird eggs. There are close to eighty-six hundred species of birds in the world, and each one lays an egg that is different from the others in size, shape, or color. Furthermore, within each species each hen lays eggs slightly different from those of the other hens.

As most eggs seem suited for the place where they rest, the external appearance of the egg itself is the first step toward minimizing the constant threat of destruction.

As a rule, the size of an egg depends on the size of the hen, so that the hummingbirds lay the smallest egg and the African Ostriches the largest. But, eggs that hatch downy birds contain more food and are larger than those that yield naked young. The Black-bellied Plover and Eastern Meadowlark are both eleven inches long, but the egg of the former, whose young are born with down, is two inches long while that of the latter is one inch.

Although a Canvasback weighs three pounds to the Ruddy Duck's one, the Ruddy lays a slightly larger egg. Ruddy hatchlings are larger than average ducklings and dive for food their first day out. Furthermore, two weeks of egg laying results in a fourteen-egg clutch weighing three pounds—a tremendous output for a one-pound hen.

Although most eggs are shaped like the chicken ovoid, some are not. The egg is shaped by the oviduct through which it passes. Probably fast-flying birds such as cormorants, swifts, and swallows lay unusually long eggs because their bodies are usually stretched out in flight. Relatively sedentary birds such as owls lay round eggs, which may be easier to turn in their nest holes. Murres lay one top-shaped egg which tends to roll in a circle rather than wandering off the precarious nest ledges. Shorebirds lay four conical eggs whose points fit together in the middle of the nest, allowing the relatively small parent to incubate all the eggs at once.

Eggs laid in concealed nests, such as those of woodpeckers, kingfishers, bee-eaters, and owls, tend to be white. Those laid in open nests are delicately tinted and covered with spots of varying sizes. The bluish eggs of the thrushes are thought to be unacceptable to taste-conscious predators.

Birds who lay their eggs on the ground generally produce something that looks like a stone, pebble, leaf, or whatever else forms the nest. The pale brown eggs of the Common Tern are spotted with dark brown to blend in with their sandy nest sites. The light gray eggs of the Piping Plover match perfectly with the dry sand on which they nest, the black spotting sparsely set to simulate the many black grains of sand. Elegant Tern eggs are boldly splotched to hide them among the bold shadows of the pebble beaches they use. The scrawlings on murre eggs are thought to serve as a means for identification in addition to camouflage. Each murre hen lays a differently tinted and marked egg, so that from hundreds of eggs resting on the ledges, each can tell which one is hers as she returns from fishing expeditions at sea.

The number of eggs per clutch varies from one in the murres and penguins to twenty for the Hungarian Partridge. Generally the clutch size increases with the dangers of nesting. The murre nesting on a cliff is safer in the long run than the partridge nesting on the

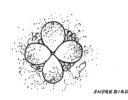

SHOREBIRD

OWL

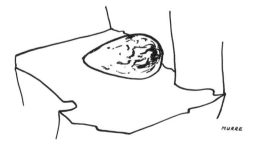

MURRE

ground. Ducks are under constant enemy surveillance from the sky above, the ground around, and the water below where fish and snapping turtles are always on the lookout for a tender pair of dangling legs. The insecurity of their life may cause them to lay eight to fifteen eggs per clutch.

The eight-pound Canada Goose lays five or six creamy-white eggs. The small number may be explained by the fact that these birds are more successful at holding their own against predators—they are larger than ducks and both parents guard the young, whereas drakes desert their mates after the eggs are laid. Also there is a tendency for the larger birds to lay fewer eggs.

Whip-poor-wills, doves, and Ruby-throated Hummingbirds lay two eggs. Most of the songbirds lay three to five. The Redwing lays two to five but usually four blue-green gems elegantly patterned with heliotrope squigglings.

Many of the birds who winter in the north, such as chickadees, nuthatches, and flickers have longer to raise their young, and lay five to ten eggs.

Songbirds lay an egg every morning until their clutch is complete. Owls, hawks, and grouse generally lay every other day. Just as diurnal birds lay every morning, so do nocturnal birds lay before midnight.

When a set is complete the average bird stops laying, as her body chemistry swings ahead into the incubation stage. If a set is destroyed, she can switch back again after four or five days and lay another. But most birds cannot keep laying indefinitely—the chicken's ability to do so having made it uniquely responsive to domestication. One flicker laid 71 eggs in 73 days trying to complete a clutch from which someone stole the final egg every day. A duck laid 363 eggs in 365 days. But such cases are exceptional, otherwise on a quiet spring morning the woods would purr with the soft thumping of emerging eggs.

The egg has many enemies besides curious people. One morning a six-foot-long cottonmouth snake slithered out of his reeds and cut the water past a man who was photographing Florida birds. Falling victim to his enemy, the snake was stretched out and opened up. Inside were found one egg belonging to a Glossy Ibis, three eggs of the Louisiana Heron, one unidentified egg, one large young Common Egret, and one adult Glossy Ibis. Apparently the last had been bitten on the head while trying to defend its egg against the deadly snake. However, young cottonmouths also serve as food for the Glossy Ibis.

Other frequent assailants are other birds. House Wrens, Common Grackles, crows, jays, and Catbirds pierce eggs with their bills and either eat the contents or leave them untouched. Long-billed Marsh Wrens are notorious enemies of Redwings, which is made more unfortunate by their habit of nesting only yards apart.

Chipmunks, squirrels, minks, weasels, and snakes are constant threats to birds who nest in the woods.

The defense mechanisms used by birds in these early stages of nesting are usually preventative. Vireos are typical of the wary birds who move a nest they know has been discovered. Some fly off to a new site, leaving the nest behind. Others dismantle the nest piece by piece and rebuild it on a new spot. Chipping Sparrows readily desert a nest with eggs if they have been attacked. Most birds will tolerate minor disturbances and hope for the best, once incubation is under way.

IX Incubation

Swimming proudly across the calm surface of a northern pond a
Horned Grebe with piercing orange-red eyes heads for a group of
onionlike reeds. Arriving at their edge she stops before a high soggy
mound of water plants six times her size. Alert, she looks around,
her rear-mounted legs nervously giving an occasional shove that
sends a little eddy of water swirling away. Satisfied with the empty
pond, she tips her head to the sky, where her eyes search for a hawk.
She sees nothing but empty blue. Quickly she slips out of the water
and pushes herself up on the mound. She snatches several billfuls of
the rotten reeds covering her eggs and lays them aside. Parting the
feathers on her abdomen, she slides onto the four greenish-white
eggs, settling her bare skin against them. Motionless she resumes incubation.

The process whereby a parent bird sits over the eggs to keep their temperature at ninety-three degrees is called incubation. At this temperature the embryo will grow. The ability of the warm-blooded bird to heat the cold egg allows birds to raise young in all parts of the world, whereas cold-blooded reptiles who are unable to heat their eggs must lay them in warm surroundings.

In Antarctica, where the temperature drops to minus seventy degrees, Emperor Penguins are able to survive the blackest winters with the egg nestled in the abdominal flap over the feet. In Florida and other hot areas the opposite form of incubation occurs by day when the parent spreads its wings over the eggs to shade them from the broiling sun. In the temperate zones, most birds apply heat by direct contact.

As a duck enters the last few days of egg laying, she begins to pluck down from her underparts. By the time the final egg is laid, she has exposed a large area of warm skin and at the same time filled her nest with down. On the nest, she parts the feathers and puts the bare skin against the eggs. When she is off the nest the down serves as a natural insulator, keeping the eggs warm for short periods.

Except for ducks, geese, and swans most birds naturally develop an incubation patch a few days before the first egg is laid. The abdominal down begins to fall out and the naked skin is suddenly supplied with extra blood. This patch only occurs in incubating individuals, including those males who habitually share incubation duties.

Ordinarily the females incubate the eggs while the males feed and guard the incubators. Such is the case among most songbirds, grouse, and ducks. But both parents incubate in the Common Tern, Chimney Swift, and Great Horned Owl as well as many others.

Males who take no part in parental duties are usually assiduous guards. But one Redwing sitting in a blueberry bush out over the water spied a large beaver swimming in his direction. He watched it until the animal was within ten feet of the bush. Amusingly the bird flew down and alighted on the massive head. Immediately the startled beaver dived with a slap that sent water four feet into the air and the nearly drowned bird back up to his post.

Aside from such amusements there are some interesting variations attached to incubation. In the Indo-Malayan region the jaçana leaves its eggs on a nest that is partly submerged in warm swamp water. It is said that an African relative takes up his lily-padded eggs under his wings to keep them warm and above water. In South America the ostrichlike rheas demonstrate a remarkable capacity for accommodation. Every dominant male has up to five or six wives in his harem, each of whom lays nine or ten eggs in the one nest. For six weeks the male incubates the resulting collection of eggs, and may guide the young for the first six weeks of their lives.

Among the other strong-legged flightless birds the incubating, brooding, and rearing of the young is also done by the male. The kiwis of New Zealand, cassowaries of Indonesia, and Common Emus of Australia are all monogamous species wherein the male does all the duties. Female emus often try to incubate until they are driven off by the persistent males, who welcome their mates back once the eggs hatch. The tinamous of South America are polygamous birds whose females appear, in some literature, to vanish into thin air after the laying of the eggs. African Ostriches are generally monogamous, but frequently nests containing the eggs of two or three females are found. Although the male does most of the caretaking, his mate often incubates by day and later accompanies the family on its peregrinations.

A really cooperative arrangement can be found in the Caribbean area with the Smooth-billed Ani. In areas where there are many birds, several females use the same large bulky nest. Every day a layer is formed as each of the five birds lays her daily egg. The layer is covered over by dead leaves, and the next day another is added, until there are four or five layers. Incubation starts at the top with several females often incubating at one time. When the top eggs hatch, the leaves are discarded and the next layer heated along with the young of the first, and so on down to the bottom.

One automatic incubator backfired for an enterprising Tree Swallow who built her nest in a tin can. It was an ideal arrangement until early summer, when the sun turned the nest into an oven and baked the life out of the occupants. Which should be cause enough for can manufacturers to make future cans of heat-reflecting aluminum.

Because eggs advanced in incubation are less expendable than those newly laid, the parents become more passionate in defending their nests as hatching nears. Songbirds swoop down at their enemies, sometimes actually hitting them, or hover a few feet above them screaming for the other birds to come, making the intruder feel unwanted. Which makes even the human being feel uncomfortable. Terns dive at the enemy, often scraping the scalp with the bill, and eject fluids from fore and aft.

A rather unique built-in defense mechanism is that used by the female hornbills of Africa who barricade themselves within the nesthole when incubation begins. Using mud, droppings, and their own secretions they close up the nest entrance until there remains only a slit large enough to admit the strong bill. Fed through the opening by the male, and able to fend off monkeys and snakes, the female stays in her nest until the young are well grown, a time that varies from six to sixteen weeks. Meanwhile she molts her feathers so that when she emerges from the hole she appears in new but drab brown plumage.

A simple but effective display is employed by most chickadees in their holes. The snake act starts when the nest entrance is blackened by an enemy. Suddenly from out of the dark silence there comes a stream of loud unrelenting hisses and reptilian gasps that would send most animals bounding on their way. The sounds are frightening to humans who are wary of snakes.

The shorebirds, most of whom nest in open areas barren of protective shrubs or trees, have the most captivating defense displays. When the eggs are nearly hatched the bird is loath to desert them until nearly walked upon. It distinguishes between two kinds of intruders: the nonpredator such as a cow, and the predator. When a cow grazes toward a nest the bird stays put until the beast is about to trample it. Then it explodes out of the grass to fly up in the oncoming face, causing it to veer away in surprise.

If the animal is predatory, the bird leaves its nest immediately and puts on an elaborate display elsewhere to lure the enemy to itself. Many shorebirds, notably the Killdeer, and the Snowy and Piping Plovers, flop around on the ground dragging their "broken" wings at convincing angles, and spreading their tails to simulate weakness. Predators will readily pursue whatever animal they think may be injured.

The Purple and Least Sandpipers, among other Arctic breeders, have the indispensable ruse of running along over the tundra like a lemming. This small rodent is the most sought-after item in Arctic diets, and the "lemming" becomes a bird again only when the enemy is far from the nest. The Piping Plover, one of the four shorebirds who nest on the beach, performs the same display by running over the sand like a mouse.

The Thick-billed or Wilson's Plover, like some other birds, has incorporated part of his courtship display in his defense. As soon as he sees an enemy approach he leaves the nest. At a distance, when sure that he is being watched, the bird begins turning around in the sand as if making a nest scrape or depression. After a moment he leaves that and runs to a new spot to make another "nest," and so on until the enemy is discouraged by inference.

The African Ostrich performs a giant shorebird display when faced with danger on the naked spaces of the veld. While the female approaches the enemy with erected feathers, dragging wing, and listing body, the male leads the young away, pursuing an erratic zigzag course until they are out of sight. Only then will the mother cease risking her life and go off in the opposite direction still feigning injury.

Many bird pairs are split up when one is killed during nesting. If the female disappears, the male loudly renews his courtship efforts until a young female hears and responds. When the male is lost the problem is slight. Most nesting areas have a bachelor population containing three or four bachelors to every mated male. This group wanders over the nesting grounds ready to supply any widow with a new male when the old fails to return. One experimenter removed ten males from a nest in ten consecutive nights. The eleventh was left in peace.

Although birds may not have intelligence as humans define it, some show amazing resourcefulness when pressed by emergencies. These are likely to survive crises that others succumb to.

A pair of Black-necked Stilts were suddenly faced with the problem of floodwaters rising around their marsh nest. After giving initial alarm cries and taking a moment for observation, they spread out over the surrounding area and began yanking up nest material, which they left on the ground, loose and available. When enough was uprooted, the hen returned to the nest, pulled the four eggs to one side, and proceeded to build up the free side with debris run to her by the male. Then she switched to the new elevation, pulling the eggs up the one inch to beneath her feet, and started to build up the lower half. The male meanwhile rushed back and forth between the nest and the outer edge of the twenty-foot-wide circle, taking tremendous strides in order to outrace the flood. As the circle diminished to within two feet of the nest, the male stopped running. He took a broad stance and began throwing the muddy leaves and twigs over his shoulders to the builder, thereby saving precious minutes. After an hour and a half, the nest was nearly five inches higher and safely beyond reach of the new water level.

Incubation continues until the last egg is hatched. The length of the period varies from the eleven days of the ground-nesting Ovenbird and parasitic cowbirds to eighty days for the large Wandering Albatross. Most songbirds incubate for twelve to fourteen days, and the waterfowl from four to five weeks.

The marked difference in the time length is partly due to size but primarily to the difference between their hatching conditions.

When incubation begins, the egg shell contains the seat of life floating on its nourishment. By the end, the embryo has absorbed all the food, as well as the lime from the shell utilized for its skeleton. With no further function to perform, the weakened shell ceases to be a protection and instead becomes a prison. To survive, the bird must make its escape.

X Hatching

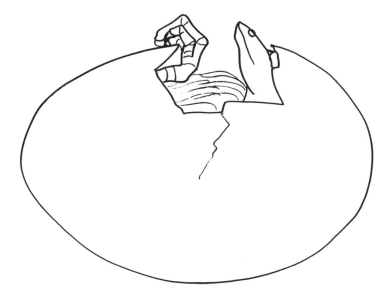

Out over the vast grasslands of Africa are thousands of umbrella-shaped trees stretching to the horizon, each one laden with a thousand hanging nests occupied by Red-billed Weavers. The birds have been incubating for thirteen days. At the end of the thirteenth day hundreds of thousands of eggs are pipped by the wakening bird within.

Early in the fourteenth day an avian population explosion is under way. A few fragments of shell fall like snowflakes to the ground below, the telltale flakes of the approaching blizzard. The shellfall intensifies until the tree zone goes white with the fragments of discarded shells burst by millions of kicking legs and straining scarlet necks. The peak lasts for several hours and then subsides as the last exhausted bee-size bodies hatch to lie crumpled in the bottoms of their nests, the products of a precisely timed community nesting cycle.

At hatching, altricial young are scarlet, naked, blind, half-formed distortions of a bird. The body is covered with loose wrinkled skin out of which may arise puffs of grayish down floating along the back, shoulders, and head. The bird consists of a very prominent rear end mounted above a swollen stomach that holds the last of the yolk, an awkward and feeble pair of legs, fragile handlike wings, and a round soft head. This sleeping life will spend its first ten days in the nest being nursed by its parents. The word altricial derives from the Latin *altrix* meaning nurse.

On the cool damp tundra just southwest of Hudson Bay, a Canada Goose and gander watch a hole being broken through the tough shell of one of their eggs. It is the twenty-ninth day of incubation. Presently the other five eggs begin to show life.

During the night and early the next day, the water-stained eggs begin to hatch. Heaving with his neck and pushing with his strong, well-developed legs, a gosling tries to force the top of the shell apart from the rest. After each exertion the bird rests for several minutes. Then the struggle begins anew. At the end of a half hour the top is rent from the body of the shell. The hatchling hooks his wet feet over the edge of the shell, and with a fierce effort pulls himself free. There he rests on his side with his rear end still in the shell and a wing and foot caught underneath.

Fifteen minutes later he pulls himself completely out of the shell, rights himself, and stands up pigeon-toed on his two feet. He rocks unsteadily forward, then rolls backward, and so finds his balance point.

His down is still very damp and clinging together at the ends. The chill breeze of the tundra sends the forlorn creature crawling under the wings of his mother, where he will dry out within an hour, to emerge a substantial fluff of olive and yellow, supported by black webbed feet, and waving his arm-wing every time he wants to move fast.

At hatching, precocial young are covered with buff or gray down, their snappy black eyes are wide open, and they are able to move under their mother in cold weather and into the shade of grasses when the sun is too hot. By the end of the day they follow their guide from the nest. These birds are precocious charmers at hatching. The name precocial comes from the Latin *coquere*, to ripen, and *prae*, before.

Altricial birds hatch in twelve days as half-formed birds who further their development in the nest. Precocial birds hatch after a month as completely formed chicks who have developed within the egg.

Hatching is an orderly process. When the hatchling first wakes up, it thrusts its bill through the inner membrane to the air sac and begins to breathe. At this stage it may start to cheep. A day later it commences to break out of its prison.

On the tip of the upper bill is a hard white spot called the egg tooth which falls off a few days after hatching. Using its neck muscles the chick rubs the egg tooth against one area of the shell until it weakens and the shell cracks in a star shape. The egg is then pipped. The hatchling rolls a bit to one side and repeats the process, making another crack next to the first. Each crack demands three or four hours of work.

During the hatchling's labors, which occur in the Redwing every five minutes or so and last as long, the egg shakes with the pulse of activity within. The tremors are barely noticeable and the tapping hardly audible, but they result in the making of five or six "stars" that go halfway round the egg at its largest point.

Throughout most of this slow process, the bird is not yet ready to emerge because the yolk sac still hangs outside his body. In the course of a day, the sac is slowly absorbed by the stomach. Almost at the moment of hatching, the last protrusion is pulled inside, and the stomach skin closed over it, thereby terminating the nourishment relation between the hatchling and the egg. The hatchling breaks through the shell and thrusts its bill out to the air.

This is its first contact with the outside world and dangers begin here. Ground-nesting birds often die within their shells as streams of ants enter the pip hole to feed on the chick held within. Tree-nesting birds suffer from similar afflictions, but most songbirds are equipped with tweezer bills that help in removing pests from their nests.

While the parents watch, the bird silently carries on the rest of his battle. Pushing hard with the amazingly strong muscles of his little body, the bird separates the two halves of his shell, so that the wide shallow end rests on his head and neck like a cap and the deeper end encases the rest of his body. Then a few moments of rest when one can see how neatly the shell comes apart.

Three or four minutes later the thrusts are renewed and the bird comes loose from the shell. He rests quietly and unmoving on his side, still two-thirds covered. The next few labors free his legs and his armlike wings. The climax comes with the final thrust when he kicks himself free of the bottom. After another rest he twists his body and flails his limbs until he rolls free of the top as well. Then he curls up as if still in the shell—his bill, handlike wings, and toes all bunched together—and rests on his side.

The shell, containing the empty remains of the hatchling's circu-

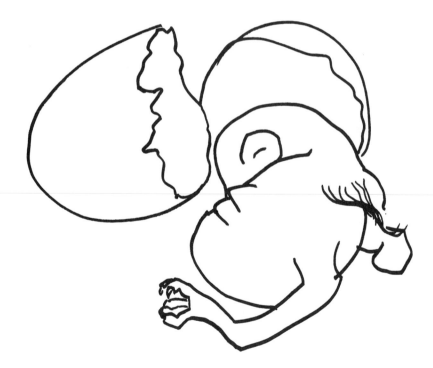

latory system as well as his first white excrement, is carried with its telltale odors far from the nest.

The whole process is an exhausting one for the hatchling and very exciting for the parents. Their role in hatching is small, as interference can rupture the blood vessels in the yolk sac or lead to other difficulties. A female English Sparrow tried removing the shell from a hatchling who had emerged but was not yet free; unwittingly she removed both shell and bird from the nest. But parents generally show interest in less fatal ways. A thrush hopped up to the rim of her nest and down again, probably torn between the instincts of brooding and feeding. After a while she flew off and returned with a worm which she offered forthwith to the still hatching egg.

So begins parental care of the young—an intensely demanding and frantic period for altricial birds, whose young charges are utterly helpless for the first ten days; a less frenzied but more drawn-out term for the parents of precocial chicks, who are able to run, swim, feed, and hide under parental guidance.

A unique and highly desirable plan of care is followed by some of the large-footed megapodes of the Australian region. The female lays her eggs in a pit that the male has dug in the ground. The male incubates them by covering them over with sun-heated vegetable debris to hold the heat for the night. Thus the eggs are incubated by the combined heat of fermentation and sunshine.

The eggs hatch several feet beneath the surface of the mound and the young use their large feet to dig their way out. From there they scurry to the nearest bush and fly into the low branches where they have some protection. The female is so busy laying eggs, and the male tending them, that they have little if any time to care for their young, who fend for themselves.

Occasionally, young are found in the mound without shells, indicating that a parent may have reburied them for protection in the night or that they returned to the mound themselves. These birds may well be the envy of those parents who actually lose weight from meeting the incessant demands of their completely helpless nestlings.

XI Altricial Young

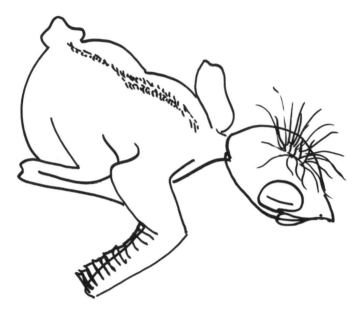

At hatching, the Redwing is an utterly helpless crumpled creature just over an inch long. His component parts are held together by a semitransparent, rose skin full of wrinkles. His partly formed head is half full of bulbous dark eyes from between which protrudes a soft wide bill. The head is supported by the nest floor and attached to the body by a loose neck, a bundle of tubes held together by skin. There are a few silky strands of pearl gray down on the head, shoulders, back, and limbs which lie on the moist skin like pieces of taffy. The legs and wings are tiny, sprawling, and almost useless. This being, once free of the egg, seems notably lacking in muscle and bone and is the essence of relaxation.

The disproportionate size and prominent positions of the yolk-filled stomach and back end of the newborn suggest the eating-evacuating-sleeping routine that marks the early days of his life. During the first few hours after hatching, the indrawn yolk is utilized by the nestling, who is too weak at first even to take food. Within that time it builds up strength with incredible speed so that feeding can begin.

Feeding follows a certain pattern. As the parents come to the nest, the landing jiggles the young into action. Their grim little mouths fly open as one, like tubular flowers bursting into bloom. Although Redwings have pink mouths, most bird gapes are bright yellow, orange, or red encircled with a yellow rim. This color spot serves as an effective target for parents bringing food to a dark nest. Excited by the open swaying mouths, the parent dives into them one after the other, the head disappearing each time. The bill touches the reflex muscle deep in the throat which causes the nestling to swallow his food automatically. So the chain of response is effected —jiggles cause gaping that stimulates feeding.

With alterations, this response sequence will be repeated as long as the family stays together. But after four days, when the nestlings are able to see, jiggles with no parents in sight mean the approach of a potential enemy, and the young will crouch in the nest. From then on the parents evoke a call, see a gape, and only then release the food. When the family leaves the nest, the food cries help locate the young for the parents, but as before they must see wide-flung mouths in order to respond.

There are several variations on this basic pattern, each determined by the basic diet of the adults whose bills are appropriately shaped.

Worms and insects form the basic diet of Redwings, warblers, wrens, and other birds having sharply pointed bills. Their horny tweezers allow the birds to delve into cracks and crannies and come out with a hiding insect. During insect hatches the young are given a tiresome lot of the emerging species. For a few days one nestful of Redstarts received mayflies almost exclusively.

During their first day of life, regardless of hatches, Black-throated Blue Warblers are given small green caterpillars, soft white grubs, and other small insects that can be handled by their delicate stomachs. From the second to the eighth days their diet is expanded to include the larger mayflies and spineless caterpillars of varying sizes. On the ninth and tenth days they are fed quantities of mayflies and dragonflies, the large hard insects.

Although feeding rates vary, most insect feeders deliver one or more insects carried in the bill to the nest every fifteen minutes or so. To feed the family, the parents must be in perpetual motion. In one day a pair of House Wrens made 491 trips to the nest. At the twelfth-day climax of a phoebe nest term, 845 trips were recorded. This same couple in seventeen days made 8942 trips. Such constant activity is very hard on the parents, who have been known to die from simple exhaustion.

The small-billed seedeaters are often unable to catch insects tiny enough for the newborn, so they predigest larger ones. A Chipping

Sparrow brought a green caterpillar to his mate, who took it in her bill and chewed it from one end to the other and back again. The male took the worm and repeated the process, then gave it back to the female who swallowed it and returned to brooding her young.

After five minutes of throaty gulpings and gapings, she reared up in the nest, put her head down into it, and pumped food into the funnel mouths of the young. Each delivery called for ten violent shakes of her body, but the one worm fed the whole brood of four.

An hour later this same mother did not take the time to predigest the delivered worm. She softened it with her bill once down the line, then crammed one end into the bright orange mouth of one nestling. The end was swallowed so she let go, expecting the rest to follow. The weight of the free end dangling from the overstuffed mouth was too great and pulled the nestling over on its face. The puzzled mother took the protruding end of the worm in her bill and pulled the bird back up on its haunches, where it took another swallow. Again she let go, and once more the baby fell over under the weight of its meal. A second time the mother pulled worm and bird back up, and the final third disappeared. The hero fell forward on his face and passed his waste to his mother, who swallowed it on the spot.

Seeds form the regular diet of the finches, whose short, solid-looking bills are designed to crush. With their gross beaks, these birds can handle most seeds and some fruits throughout the year, but in summer they thrive on the abundance of insects. The parents first soften the seeds by storing them in the throat. At the nest, the parent puts the whole bill into the diminutive throat and regurgitates the appropriate amount. This storehouse type of feeding is much easier on the parents, as several young can usually be fed in one trip.

The Cedar Waxwing feeds its young three times an hour, much less than most birds, where thirty feedings is more normal. It has the ability to bring up a softened berry often enough to make one trip last for several rounds.

Hawks and owls live on the flesh of animals, which they carry in their sharply hooked beaks and talons and eviscerate with one swoop of either. Rodents, snakes, or small birds are brought to the nest where they are initially fed in small pieces to the young. After a few days, the young are able to cut their own meat.

Most hawks are fed every six hours or so. Owls sometimes wait ten or twelve hours between feedings—they must regurgitate a pellet of fur and bones before they can eat more mice. These birds sometimes go several days without food, but when hunting is good, food is stored in the nest. Such a cache was found in the nest of four Barn Owls who were hoarding seventy-three mice.

Eagles nesting in the northern interior subsist mainly on the abundant small mammals such as rabbits, muskrats, and woodchucks. Southern eagles tend to inhabit areas near water where their fish diet is readily available. Occasionally eagles will attack and kill weakened wildfowl but generally they stick to the more easily killed animals and fresh carrion.

One curious aspect of predatory feeding is the tendency for the Goshawk of Europe to select from a flock victims of atypical coloring. Under controlled experiments, the hawk tended to choose those pigeons who were in the minority as to color, thus carrying out nature's design to eliminate those who are different from the majority.

An avian instance of majority rule and minority right seems to be at work on Gardiners Island, New York, where Ospreys have retreated before the invasion of marauding sea gulls. Gangs of gulls have so harried adult Ospreys carrying fish to their nests that raising young Ospreys has become impracticable. In 1940 the island meadows contained one hundred active nests and the forest another two hundred. By 1961 there were a handful on the meadows and the forest nests were drastically reduced in numbers.

Aerial insects are the diet of the swifts and swallows. Swifts, unlike their hummingbird relatives, are gradually losing their bills and gaining huge mouths instead. The small bills are surrounded by bristles which help trap insects as the birds swoop openmouthed through swarms of insects, scooping up their food as they go. As the insects stream in, they are gathered into little food balls, each containing up to one hundred individuals, and stored in the throats. At the nest the food is apportioned out in long intervals, rationed against the time when bad weather keeps the insects grounded and the swifts are unable to eat.

Swift nestlings are able to survive long fasts by falling into torpidity when their temperature drops to below fifty degrees. In this state they can last ten days, although one unusually strong bird survived three weeks without food. Swallows and nighthawks also feed in this grandiose manner of swirling through their food supply and then going home to savor it.

The formation of some birds' feeding apparatus would seem to present feeding problems, but it does not. The hummingbirds feed their young predigested nectar and insects, jabbing their spearlike bill deep into the throats of the young who, like the sword-swallower, must elongate their necks to avoid being run through. Herons have a less efficient but satisfactory way of transferring food. The young one grabs the bill of the parent in its own at right angles and shakes it to release the food. The partly digested fish and lizards come up from the crop and spill into the young throat. Adult pelicans store their fish in the crop, fly to the young, stretch their necks and open their bills so the young can go in after it.

Birds feed their young in a certain order, beginning with the highest-reaching, noisiest one. This usually works well, as after a feeding the normal bird settles back into a deep sleep that gives the others a chance to be fed. But occasionally one or two insatiable members will clamor incessantly for food, a survival technique used by cowbirds and Old World cuckoos, and unless the parents are observant the weaker ones are likely to be buried under the trampling feet of their brothers and neglected. This may be another stage at which nature weeds out the weak so the strong may be stronger.

Most birds are said to be unobservant in the matter of feeding. But one male Yellowthroat made an effort to set things right. He arrived at the nest while his mate was away and fed two of the young himself. When the female returned with a bug, he reached out to take the meal from her. Stubbornly she withheld it and gave it to the bird last fed. Quickly the male retrieved the insect and put it down the throat of the third nestling.

Birds do not waste their food, nor are the young forced to eat what they do not need. If food is not swallowed as soon as it is

ONE DAY OLD

TWO DAYS

AT HATCHING

TEN DAYS

NINE DAYS

EIGHT DAYS

THREE DAYS

FOUR DAYS

DEVELOPMENT

OF THE

REDWING

WITHIN

THE

NEST.

FIVE DAYS

SIX DAYS

SEVEN DAYS

given, it is withdrawn from the mouth and given to the next. That is, unless the unwanted portion is attached to a portion already swallowed.

The feeding stimulus is very highly developed in some birds, such as the one who brought food to her young still unhatched. As birds get older they begin to cry for food, a stimulus that cannot be ignored by most mothers. In one case two Robins sharing a mate built their nests next to one another. When the young of the first mate were ready to leave the nest, the eggs of the second were just hatching. Both hens had to feed their young, but the stimulus from the noisy older birds was so much stronger than the silent cries of the newborn that both parents fed the adolescents and left the babies to perish.

Among songbirds, nest sanitation is exemplary, their nests being generally, though not always, immaculate. After each feeding, the parents anticipate what is inevitable and place their bills near the tail of the nestling. The nestling elevates his already prominent rear end and passes a white fecal sac to the waiting bill. If no sac is forthcoming the parent prods the end with its bill to stimulate the movement.

The sac is a gelatinous mucous membrane enclosing the limy white waste. Because of the speed with which food passes from one end of the bird to the other, it is incompletely digested. During the first three to five days of the nest cycle, the parents usually swallow the sacs, probably deriving some nourishment from them. After that they carry the sacs from the nest, thereby helping to avoid detection by predators.

For the first five or six days of nest life, the young are naked and cold-blooded. To keep them warm, the mother sits over them as she sat over her eggs. She broods them eighty percent of the time, tapering off as the young gain strength and need more food.

The brooding instinct binds the mother to her young wherever their nest is placed. An Eastern Phoebe returning to her porch nest at night, overshot, and flew into a lighted cabin kitchen. Unable to get the bird outdoors again, the owner solved the problem by bringing the nest into the kitchen and placing it up on a shelf. The room was vacated for the night. The following morning the phoebe was on her nest. When the door was opened she flew up on the log wall, took one look at the woods beyond, and shot out of the house. The nest was back on its former site by the time she returned with the overdue first meal of the day.

Most parents share the chores of parenthood. Both parents bring food to the young, and when the female is absent from the nest, the male gives food to them. Most males try to feed the young even when the mother is there, so strong is their instinct. Often their efforts are discouraged by their mates and they become henpecked husbands. One particularly "thwarted" Scarlet Tanager began pecking his eight-day-old birds as well as their mother, instead of feeding them, so his mate was forced to drive him off.

The availability of food is a factor determining the size of bird families. When food is short, a few birds seem to lay fewer eggs than usual. In the year following the lemming emigrations, the lemming-eating Snowy Owl and Rough-legged Hawk are less abundant on their breeding grounds and lay fewer eggs than normal. The Rough-legged Hawk raises six young in good lemming years, but only three in off years. The Barn Owl can breed most of the year when meadow mice are abundant, but when they are scarce the owls may even skip a year.

Year after year insectivorous birds hatch their young when insects are most abundant and there is food to go around. Stomach examinations show tremendous individual need and capacity for food. The stomachs of four large nighthawks held 500 mosquitoes, 2175 flying ants, and 34 May beetles; 24 cloverleaf weevils; 375 ants, and 340 grasshoppers; 52 bugs, 3 beetles, 2 wasps, and a spider. Multiply each stomach by four and there is one family's consumption. A flicker ate 28 white grubs, which multiplied by ten equals a family meal. One Swainson's Hawk held more than 200 grasshoppers and crickets, which quadrupled represents a family intake.

In order to understand the voracious appetite of the eating and sleeping nestling, he must be regarded simply as a growing adolescent. He hatches weighing about six percent of what he will weigh when he learns to fly. In eleven days the Redwing develops from a helpless naked inchling to a flying feathered four-inch squawker. His growth is phenomenal.

The nest term allows the bird to develop first the body, then the feathers and heat control, and lastly some coordination. The first four days in the nest show tremendous daily increase in the bird's size. The next five days are a period of feather explosion, when most of the energy goes into covering the angular frame. During the last two or three days the bird becomes much more coordinated.

At hatching, the bird is much like an insect emerging from its pupa—it is damp and still except for the legs, which grope periodically to change position. The head and neck rest on the floor of the nest until the hatchling is able to gape for food. Even then the head can be held up only for a few seconds before it slowly returns to the floor as energy fails.

By the end of the first day the bird is larger and stronger. The limbs are held in, rather than hanging loosely, and the bird is able to maneuver ninety degrees of a circle in an effort to reach shade. The most definite movement when disturbed is the strong curling and uncurling of the toes. On the water the nestling floats, listing to one side.

After the second day the bird is much larger again. The feather sheaths begin to turn the feather tracts blue and actually emerge on the outer wing. The bird is able to pivot in search of a warm nestmate and to right himself. In the water he is able to float with his limbs spread evenly over the water, maintaining an even keel.

When three days old the body is much larger and the legs are longer and stronger. The wing feather sheaths are well out. The bird is very relaxed in the water, may swim a foot or so, collide with a reed, rest his head on it, and gape for food.

After four days the body is much larger and the feather explosion begins, with the slate-gray sheaths starting to push out all over the body. The eyes are large slits and the nestling is able to hold his head up for a few seconds. He also can crawl more or less continuously with both wings and legs going. In the water he paddles frantically with all four limbs, tires, sputters, and starts to go under.

On his fifth birthday the bird is still larger and very awkward—his wings are longer and his feet very large but they lack coordination. The wing quills are ¾-inch long and the spine is prominently defined by a thatch of stiff little quills. With his eyes partly open, the nestling crawls about constantly with his head up, but every few seconds it drops. He swims fast with his head high out of water, but when he tires the head drops and the bird submerges.

At six days the legs are much longer. The wing quills are an inch long, and feather sheaths are well out over the rest of the body. The feet are stronger and are able to grip the nest bottom and the fingers, the first sign of perching ability. With his eyes half open the bird swims awkwardly with his head and neck well out of water like a snake. Upon reaching sticks he is unable to climb up on them, but at no point does he start to sink.

After seven days the bird has lost his naked look. The wing feathers are ¼-inch long, and the other feathers are pushing out from the tips of their casings. The bird swims with more confidence to some sticks and climbs up on them until only his back end is in the water. He clings well but cannot go farther.

When eight days old the bright-eyed bird perches smartly on his feet, looking feathered for the first time. The wing feathers are out ⅓-inch and the breast feathers curve, giving the bird his first contours. The feet grip effectively so that the normal enemy would have some difficulty removing him from the nest. He swims easily to sticks, climbs three or four inches out of water and clings doggedly, calling for help.

The ninth day produces a young bird in all respects. Although he teeters a bit, the nestling perches like a proper bird with his head up and tail down. His angular frame is hidden beneath the contours of chocolate and buff feathering which gives him a nearly finished look. Afloat, the nestling swims excitedly to the sticks and crawls up through them toward the nest, calling loudly for the parents, and shivering all the while. Some individuals may leave the nest on this day.

By the end of the tenth day the bird is well feathered except for the jowls and top of the breast. The pins on the forehead are the only ones left to burst. The bird flies from the nest when disturbed but may calm down and return.

During the eleventh day he is able to fly several yards at a time. So the fledgling leaves the nest for its surroundings, an appealing reminder of what amazing developments can take place in twenty-seven cubic inches while, unobserving, the rest of the world paddles by.

The wing feathers of most songbirds have sprung their sheaths by the sixth or seventh day in the nest, so that the last few days are spent preening. But the feathers of burrow-nesting species like the kingfishers do not unsheath until the young are ready to leave the burrow. This delay protects the delicate tips from being prematurely worn away by the dirt walls.

Baby birds, because of their size and nakedness, are prone to a number of enemies, some of which they will later eat. Small parasites, such as lice, are the death of young whose mothers fail to de-louse their nests. One Myrtle Warbler in thirteen minutes ate 250 lice in her nest. The male picked lice off his legs and, in a fit of economy characteristic of nature, fed them to the young.

Ants and maggots have been known to attack and kill babies. Nestlings hatched next to tent caterpillars will feast if they precede the worms. But when the worms appear before the young, they may swarm through the nest, smothering the tiny occupants.

The Purple Grackle is notorious for its eating habits. One July evening a grackle was causing much disturbance in a colony of Red-wings. Opposed by the many who heckled him, he walked up the lakeshore toward the territory of a lone Catbird scolding near her nest. When the grackle came opposite the territory, the Catbird went into a clump of blueberry bushes and continued scolding. The grackle then turned in and walked the five yards to the bush from which the mewing came, and disappeared. For the following three or four minutes the frenzied cries of the Catbird told the lake community that her nestlings were being threatened. After a final piercing scream there was silence. A minute later the grackle reappeared on the shore and flew off across the darkening lake.

Although snakes, chipmunks, squirrels, and birds take their toll of hatchlings, the most common enemy of all songbirds is the cowbird.

The irresponsible human mother who neglects her baby hoping that someone else will bring it up for her has her counterpart in the bird world. In the Old World, cuckoos are the most skilled at shunning responsibility; in the New World, cowbirds are such mothers. Because their young are raised in foster homes at the expense of the rightful young, such birds are known as brood parasites.

Cowbirds lay most of their eggs in the nests of vireos, small buntings such as the Song Sparrow, and warblers. The eggs of these birds are small so the cowbird egg usually does not lack incubation from being lost under larger ones. Their feeding habits are identical with those of the cowbird, which increases the nestling's chances of survival. Finally, these birds are all mild in temperament, inclining them to accept the strange egg and its hatchling.

The cowbird finds her foster nests by watching them being built. The sight of nest building helps stimulate her so she lays her egg at approximately the same time the host lays hers. Knowing in advance whose nests she will parasitize, the cowbird flies onto a different one each day, deposits her egg in a few seconds around 5 A.M., and departs before the owner comes to lay hers. Each time she lays an egg, she must remove one egg of the host's if there are two or more. This she does the day preceding or following the laying of her own, which sometimes results in the eating of another cowbird's egg. Often two or three females will choose the same nest for parasitizing when there are not enough to go around.

Each female probably lays four or five eggs, but one captive laid thirteen eggs in fourteen days. The incubation period lasts eleven days, shorter than most birds, so that ideally the egg hatches a day or two before those of the host. This gives it a monopoly on food brought to the nest and speeds its growth. If by some freak of timing the cowbird lays her egg after the host has commenced to incubate, the cowbird may be too small to be fed along with the older hosts and will perish in turn.

Young cowbirds are not prone to throwing the rightful young out of the nest as cuckoos do. Usually each cowbird is raised at the expense of one host young, but this depends on the ability of the parents to cope with a crowd. The fact that the cowbird hatches larger than the host young and increases its weight by one hundred percent during the first two days accounts for its survival success, as size alone frequently causes the crowded bird to shove the others out.

At hatching, the cowbird weighs 2.5 grams. By the end of the second day he is up to 8 grams. After nine days he is thirteen times his hatching weight, at 33 grams. The monstrous initial increase gives him a headstart over the host young whose growth does not show until the third and fourth days. Later his growth rate diminishes to 5.5 percent the last day. He usually leaves the nest a day or two before any others who might have managed to survive his company.

The cowbird's seeming independence is demonstrated by his inability to respond to the alarm cries of his foster parents. In spite of this he stays near the nest for two or three days, and in the nest vicinity for another four days, soliciting care from the enslaved foster parents who continue to feed him for another two weeks. Often this persists for a whole month as the sight of parents stimulates the highly capable fledgling to clamor for more food, and some of the parents are unable to resist.

Toward the end of July the young begin flocking for the post-juvenal molt, gathering in groups of hundreds. After the molt they join the adults in the marshes, a feat that seems remarkable considering that most cowbirds have had no previous experience with others of their kind.

Occasionally a mother cowbird comes to the foster nest and feeds her own bird. Such behavior suggests that the cowbird retains the maternal instinct and enjoys her young so long as someone else bears the responsibility.

Of the 149 forms of birds who are imposed upon by the cowbird, only the Robin and Catbird regularly destroy the egg by piercing it and carrying it off. The Yellow Warbler usually builds a new nest on top of the polluted one. Nests of three tiers are common and nests of five have been found, but these would seem to take more energy than they are worth. Many desert their nests. But such unfriendly acts are more rare than usual—most birds accept the strange egg—so cowbirds continue to flood our countryside and rid our cattle of their parasites.

When nests become crowded, the growing occupants show increasing eagerness to leave home. Songbirds spend the last third of their nest life restlessly moving around while their feathers shoot out of their sheaths. When one begins to stretch, it is the signal for the others to follow suit. The wings are elevated above the head and the muscles slowly stretched to their limit, then relaxed as the wings are brought back to the sides. A bird poised on the nest rim will also stretch his wing and leg over the side, a gesture that precedes wing-lifting.

Birds jostle each other within the nest and occasionally push a rimsitter overboard—these unfortunates may be cared for by the parents as long as they survive. Grounded eaglets are left to fend for themselves. The jostling ordinarily bursts the seams of the nest. Meadowlarks flail their nest apart the day before they leave and the parents are forced to protect them from sun and rain.

People used to think that these exercises were actually preparation for flight, but when the wings of some nestlings were bound until nest-leaving they flew off without faltering.

Young eagles in their treetop go through weeks of practicing for life. At one month they begin to feed themselves, grasping fish left in the nest and ripping them open with their beaks. In the next two weeks the eaglets take up wing exercises like other birds. But with such large wings control is more difficult. First one is stretched out to the side, then the other. At six weeks both wings are tried. One eaglet confidently put both wings out at once, but lacked sufficient strength to bring them back in. While he decided what to do, the wings rocked back and forth on their tips. The problem was solved by his bringing the body out to the stranded wingtips, first stepping out to the left tip, then back to the right.

When eaglets are not resting they practice hunting techniques. They break nest sticks with their powerful feet and pounce on twig rabbits. At eleven weeks, periodic wing-flapping becomes a rhythmic beating that can lift the birds off their perch. Gradually they start flying to perches above the nest where, standing still and holding on, they practice hovering. At twelve weeks, they fly a hundred yards or so to join their parents at the off-nest perch.

The length of the nesting period varies according to the size of the bird and the location of the nest. Eagles stay in the treetop nest for three months so they can attain full size and be able to fly from their towers on the first attempt. Redwings nest for ten or eleven days, when they are able to fly short distances into nearby bushes.

Within the Tanager Family the length of nesting period varies from one species to another, depending on where they nest. Ground-nesters leave their exposed nests after eleven to thirteen days. Open tree-nests are less dangerous, so the young stay for sixteen to twenty days. Hole nests are safest and house their families for twenty-three days. These periods are more or less typical of most birds nesting in similar situations.

Birds who nest on the ground are in constant danger of discovery from the time of hatching. But when the young begin calling their parents at the age of five days the nests become obvious and leave-taking is accomplished as soon as possible. Ovenbirds hop out one at a time on the eighth day, each young following a parent into the shelter of the unknown.

Birds who nest above ground stay longer. Tree-nesting songbirds commonly leave after ten days to two weeks. Woodpeckers stay in their holes for nearly a month and are accomplished fliers at take-off. Swallows and swifts also have elevated homes from which they must make safe exits, as they are unable to fly if they fall on the ground. Their wings are so long and their feet so small for clinging to walls that they cannot get takeoff lift. Like the woodpeckers, they stay in or around their safe nest-holes for three weeks to a month. Dipper nests are often located in a rocky crevice behind a waterfall. The young leave after twenty-five days and fly through the waterfall or cross a rushing stream before landing safely for the first time.

The actual process of nest-leaving varies. When disturbed, the young explode out of their nest, flying with their half-grown wings and running with their long, lanky legs, making an elusive if not very clever getaway. Normally, nest-leaving is quiet and secretive.

The young of herons and owls vary in age, so while one clambers over neighboring branches, another is cowering unfeathered in the nest. Songbird young are the same age and leave the same day.

The day before leaving, the bravest birds respond to their parents' calls by fluttering out to the branch next to the nest, if there is one.

All day they hop in and out of the nest with great excitement, courage, and then doubt.

A detailed report of what takes place in a nest of Eastern Phoebes is probably typical of "the day before" for most birds. After the first morning feeding is over, the mother calls a few *pheeps*, which the young recognize as the signal to get out of the nest. They lift their heads and begin beating their wings on the nest. The mother returns and feeds one, then departs calling.

Within seconds, one bird hops from the nest to the rafter. The others turn toward him and gape, suddenly realize he is not a parent, and settle back. The hero beats his wings, preens, and silently nibbles his nestmates, who are still in the nest.

The mother calls and flies in to feed another nestling. The outsider returns to the nest uttering little cries. The nestmates bill each

other for a minute, then preen their feathers with meticulous care. The mother calls again and the nestlings fall silent, but remain alert.

Five minutes later the mother feeds the brave one and takes his sac. As she flies off, the young renew their wing-stretching and preening. The former hero now sits on the nest rim and seems unable to depart again, although staying on the rim is obviously difficult and risky. Ten minutes later he finally hops off the nest for several seconds and returns. The parents call. The young lean out of the nest, then settle back.

Suddenly the brave one is out again. The mother calls and he answers, wobbles on his legs, and beats his wings fast. Very much in the spirit of the moment the mother swoops in and out from the nest site, which results in two more birds braving the dreaded rafter. The three young beat their wings with intense excitement while uttering sweet rattles, then subside into preening. The fourth bird crouches in the nest, unable to join the others beyond.

After five minutes the others return to the nest. The mother flies past and her brood show no positive response. She returns to feed one and take the sac. Three minutes later she repeats until all are fed, but sacs are not taken from the last four feedings. Meanwhile the hero has perched himself on the nest rim. As a result of the pushing and shoving of the crowded birds, the rimsitter slips reluctantly off his perch, catches the edge of the beam, and falling backward into space beats his undersized wings frantically for half a minute before regaining his balance and composure on the beam.

The birds start leaving their nest early in the morning. The parents fly back and forth encouraging their brood with winning cries and cheeps. The nestful get very excited, and the bravest are suddenly inspired to take off, flutter wild-eyed up to the nearest branch or down to the ground, and freeze motionless as their tiny hearts pound away. The less brave huddle together and listen to their clamorous parents, who periodically fall quiet, as if to give the young a breathing spell. After an hour of sympathetic huddling and billing, the third suddenly leaps into space and is followed by the fourth, who does not wish to be left behind.

Sometimes a frightened nestling must be coaxed from the nest with food, cries of all sorts, and flight-passes. If such efforts do not work, the parents desert the doubting Tom in order to care for the other fledglings. A young Red-eyed Vireo finally dived off its deserted nest, fluttered at constantly decreasing altitude across a path, and dropped into the leaves on the ground. But there was no sign of his family.

A more normal nest-leaving was heralded by a pair of Cardinals voicing alarm notes in the yard. One of the two young had left the nest and hidden itself in a carissa bush twenty feet away. Within a half hour the other one, tired of being left unattended, hopped from the nest and started off in the other direction, clambering over the thorny orange branches close to its nest. The parents immediately took notice and flew to its aid, squealing encouragement. Ten minutes later the fledgling took new heart and leaped from the nest tree, landing on the ground with spread wings and upturned bill.

It advanced with three-foot-long teetering flights to the base of a tree forty feet from the nest, accompanied by the ringing-voiced parents. All along his route they swooped down next to him and flew back into the branches above, urging their explorer to return to a tree branch.

Arriving at his preferred tree, the small bird seemed very alarmed by the parental excitement and wild from its new experiences. At the trunk he hopped to a clinging position about eight inches above ground. From there the father guided him with short swift flights into the dense middle foliage. With their young in hiding, both parents became quiet and turned their attention to feeding them, which was still done by regurgitation. After two or three revival feedings, the parents went back to their nuptial tree where they could watch over their separated charges.

A young Red-bellied Woodpecker launched himself from his nest-hole far out over a road. Beating his wings desperately, he flew straight up the middle of the road toward an approaching car. The bird was unable to alter his course or gain altitude as the situation demanded. So the driver, sensing the drama of the event, veered his car out of the way, and the fledgling continued unabashed as far as the curve. This he could not negotiate either, so he ended up sprawling in the underbrush, panting with the challenge-victory of his first half-minute abroad.

Because of the inevitable excitement and disturbance created, nest-leaving is a time of great danger. Occasionally a bird is injured in the drop from its home. But the great danger comes from the simple inexperience of fledglings, who must learn life the hard way, the only way. Suddenly they leave behind the relatively secure nest and encounter the rough world of leaves, twigs, living food, and enemies. Some are eager to explore while others are doubtful and forget that to stay in one place too long is in itself dangerous.

After leaving the nest, all young birds are separated for the sake of silence, the greatest protection in nature. Each is taken by a parent into the leaves where they will spend the next few days hiding and gaining practical knowledge about the world around them. The birds move in circles around the general vicinity of the nest so they are seldom seen in the same place twice. While the young continue growing, their wings and tails lengthening to functional size, they are cared for by their knowing parents.

The first lessons learned are in safety and obedience. Because enemies are ever present, the birds are not allowed to peep except for food—which brings prompt reply. Young birds can be eaten by any larger animal they meet. Young Marsh Wrens and Redwings fall prey to other marsh animals like turtles, bullfrogs, and even fish if the birds somehow land in the water. Swallows and humming-birds are sometimes swallowed by fish who mistake them for large flies when they skim the water to drink.

Mortality rates among young birds soar during the first months out of the nest. In Europe eighty-five percent of the tits, the European chickadee, die before the year is out. In Africa nearly fledged Red-billed Weavers are in equal proportions as to sex, whereas adult males outnumber the females three to one. In the United States it is estimated that less than a third of the fledglings manage to survive their first year, but their chances increase with age and experience.

While the young are learning to conceal themselves, they are also beginning to fly, if they did not leave-nest in flight. It takes most songbirds two weeks to fly, during which time they are fed by their parents. Although the motions of flying are inborn, hard muscles and the refinements of flight can only be acquired through practice. Once this mobility is attained, the family reunites. The young accompany their parents through a week or two of adult life, learning where and how to capture their food, as well as other details necessary to bird existence.

The parents desert the young when they have become more or less self-sufficient and the free birds complete their growth afterward. Ovenbirds are independent at five weeks. They leave the nest at eight days and hop their way through the next three. From eleven to twenty days they begin flying; from twenty to thirty days they feed themselves somewhat, and finally serve a short apprenticeship prior to scattering. Chickadees feed themselves at twenty-six days but do not leave their parents until seven weeks old.

Robins leave their parents after one month, while their buff breasts are still covered with dark spots. One such bird was encountered in the woods one July morning. He flushed out from the leaves, where he was invisible, up onto a tree branch, and landed in the camouflaging position with his gray back to his enemy. After a moment he turned and revealed his eye-catching front instead. Subsequently, he showed signs of a conflict between flying off and staying put, fascinated by man-made squeaks. The dilemma was solved by his once more turning his back to the stranger, whom he continued to watch from over his shoulder. Such confused responses would have meant early death had the enemy been hunting.

The average natural life-span for small birds, considering the enormous losses suffered during nesting and adolescence, is less than two years. Experts owe the breeding success of the Red-billed Weaver to three factors: the eggs hatch simultaneously, the birds usually do not nest in the same area twice, and the young breed when less than a year old. If songbirds could learn the weaver way our forests would have shellfalls in June.

XII *Precocial Young*

Where the altricial bird demands much care for a short time, the precocial bird needs little care for a long time. From hatching on, life is a series of encounters with enemies, vegetation, and food, for he is born in a nest on the ground from which he ventures fourth almost immediately after birth. Life may appear to be easier because he can move, but it can be cut short before he even gets his head out of the door.

In early July, a Common Tern kicks free of its ant-ridden shell and throws its exhausted, contorted body onto the Cape Cod sand. Its slick wet down clings to its fragile frame, its pale legs are drawn up to its body, and its toes are clenched in pain. The body is pulled into a ball, the eyes still closed, trying to escape from the ants that stand all over it sinking their fangs into its flesh. Shrunken up in muscular convulsions, this creature is losing a long and hopeless battle.

Next to him lies a pipped egg with a stream of ants crawling in and out of the hole, which reveals a chick unborn, already dead. The parents do not have bills small enough to pick up ants, so are unable to help.

Six feet away, resting in the shade of sea grass, is another tern fluffed out—beige down streaked with chocolate—and blending perfectly with the shadows around him. By the time the ants discover him, his strong legs can carry him out of their reach.

Precocial chicks who hatch on a sunny day are clothed in a halo of down by the end of one hour. The sunshine strikes the tip of each down feather, turning it into pale gold. The down is most dense where most needed—on the backs of land birds and on the stomachs of water birds. This retains some heat, which gives the chick a degree of control over its temperature. But during chilly weather, the chick must be brooded.

By the time the down is dry, the chicks' eyes are open and the oversize legs functioning well. Surrounded by her peeping young, the precocial mother leaves the nest as soon as all the eggs are hatched and the young dry and rested. When hatching continues into the night, the departure is postponed until the following morning. Most of the young waddle from their nest behind their mother, geese being led by the gander and followed by the goose. Semi-precocial birds, such as gulls and terns, spend several days near their nests, which are protected in part by the colony.

Goldeneyes and Wood Ducks perform spectacular exits from their tree nest-holes up to sixty feet above ground. When the young are dry, the duck flies to the ground and cries for her young to follow. Using their unusually sharp claws, the young climb up the sides of the nest-hole and appear in the entrance. One by one they leap into space and drop to earth, where they bounce once or twice and land on their feet. From there the troop moves single file down through the woods to the lake where they will grow up.

Loons, grebes, and swans either follow their parents from the nest and swim behind them, or are given a ride on the parents' backs; adult loons and grebes sink down into the water so the young do not have to climb so far, and signets are often lifted up by the elevator foot of the parent.

Feeding begins immediately. Land birds such as plovers, rails, and grouse can feed themselves from the start if the parents show them where food is found. Some surface-feeding ducks, such as Mallards, Blacks, and teals, are able to glean the water's surface of small insects. But the diving ducks, loons, and grebes must wait patiently on the surface, pretending to feed, while their parents dive to the bottom for minute lake-bottom animals.

Implied in all that young birds do is an awareness of danger. The chicks are covered with camouflage-down at birth which makes them very difficult to see, even when their exact position is known. All birds learn to freeze when they hear the alarm note; young sand-colored Skimmers play dead with limp hanging head when they are picked up, a condition that would render them useless to predators who must see their meals alive at capture. Baby Piping Plovers are also colored like the dry sand beneath them, small silvery puffballs with large black eyes that resemble pebbles when open and sand when shut in the attitude of defense.

Baby loons and grebes cling to the parental back as the adult deflates its air sacs and submerges submarinelike into the lake.

Large families like ducks and grouse respond to the alarm cry differently. They scatter in all directions to confuse the enemy, then freeze in hiding where they land. If a small fleet of mergansers is moving downstream and the duck suddenly cries, the young explode silently into the reeds and freeze with eyes shut so the camouflage will be nonreflecting and perfectly still. When necessary, the duck stays in the foreground to distract the enemy. When danger is past, the mother sounds the all-clear signal and the ducklings reassemble with obvious delight and continue on their way.

Such large families are kept together by a strongly developed social bond. If a chick is lost, it peeps and the whole family searches for it until it is found. This bond lasts only as long as it is needed, until the young are ready for independence.

Young birds attain flight when they are half the size of the adults.

Land birds, for whom flight for escape is usually necessary, fly in two to four weeks, water birds between six and twelve weeks. Goslings grow flight feathers while their parents are in the flightless postnuptial molt, a time when the whole family escapes attention by remaining quiet and well hidden. By six or seven weeks, or mid-August in the north, the adults have new feathers and the young have reached the flight stage so the family is again able to venture into the open. The young continue their apprenticeship for another week or two before the family disperses.

Canvasbacks usually hatch in late June and take immediately to open water, whereas surface ducks such as Mallards stay near the shore. The families feed and travel at twilight and spend their days sitting quietly on the water, as far as possible from shore. As soon as their down is dry, the young are able to dive, but they tire so readily that a persistent enemy might get his due. For the first two weeks they feed on the surface, snatching flying insects and taking whatever food is shown them by their mother. After that they start diving for food and are able to make three or four consecutive dives and swim underwater.

Canvasback mothers are likely to abandon their growing young when faced with an enemy. At such times ducklings often band with older ducks—one White-winged Scoter led such a group of eighty-four ducklings less than two weeks old.

Under normal circumstances the young are deserted, regardless of age, during the first week of August, which allows time for the hen to complete her molt before ice sets in. With flight a month away the young band together, the older ones guiding the younger, with various species of diving ducks sometimes intermixing. These youth groups are much less wary and venturesome than they were with their mothers. Flight is gradually achieved between nine and eleven weeks of age.

The following history of a Ruffed Grouse family shows what can happen in the course of one year. A mother led her ten chicks from the nest, leaving behind one egg that failed to hatch. She taught them about feeding, then about getting under cover when she sounded the alarm. But as sometimes happens, the young did not learn their lessons well enough and the following list of tragedies occurred.

One was taken by a Sharp-shinned Hawk, another got lost and presumably froze to death, three were missing after a skunk barged into the family group, and one was lost to a Cooper's Hawk. Four of the ten survived until the family breakup in the fall.

The tragedy was completed in the months to follow. One was shot by a hunter. The mother and one young died during the harsh winter, and an unwary male was taken off his drumming log by a fox the following spring. One female and the original father were left at the end of the year, an incestuous and unlikely potential for carrying on the grouse population into the next year.

XIII Independence

A family of Cardinals flies through the trees along the beach, two parents with their two young. The parents are slightly larger than their offspring, whom they feed only occasionally in response to food cries and gaping. Apparently the young are large enough to fend for themselves and the parents are being used as crutches.

The following day the scene changes. The young male flies to his father and cries for food with spreading wings and gaping. The father, instead of responding with the usual concern, flies at the young one with poised feet and emits scolding notes characteristic of a bird defending his territory. The fledgling is confused and flies out of his father's way, lands nearby, quietly collects himself, and repeats his plea for food. Again the father flies at his offspring as male to male with harsh scolding notes, erected crest, and feet held out to drive him off. The begging bird retreats, is quiet, and cries. A third time the old male flies at the young and lashes out at him with feet and wings.

Finally the young male "understands," flicks his tail as a bird who belongs elsewhere, and departs from the scene to a nearby tree. There he perches for several minutes flicking his tail and watching his aggressive father. At last he leaves the area. The mother does the same to her charge in another part of the area some hours later. And the young have achieved independence.

If the young do not leave the parents when they are able, then the parents leave the young, for in nature families separate so the members can perpetuate.

Most songbirds scatter peacefully because the young have each other to lean on and generally form flocks with other young. Red-wings are driven off when their parents settle down to raise a second brood, the young flocking in bands that cruise around the marsh.

Ruffed Grouse young scatter in the fall, first the cocks, then the hens, each wandering for miles through the woodland in search of habitat unclaimed by others.

Shorebird adults leave their feathering young in July and start south without them.

Among those birds who raise only one or two young, parting is more dramatic. Grebes peck their offspring in an effort to drive them away, sometimes only to see a reluctant juvenile drop dead at their feet from overpecking.

A proverb points out that a bird must crawl to the edge of the cliff before it can fly, and so some must. The Slender-billed Shearwaters are deserted by their parents when fourteen weeks old. After a one-week fast the young move out of their nest-burrows, perhaps old rabbit homes, and waddle to the cliff under cover of night, take a long look, and leap into the sea. Murres and puffins are likewise deserted by their parents, and after one week of starvation on their high cliffs, they too are forced by hunger to join the fish.

Gannets starve their six-week-old young for ten days to three weeks, when the young dive off the ledge. They plummet into the cold sea and swim off, living the next ten days on fat accumulated before the starvation period. During the swimming period their flight feathers grow out. Thereafter they are able to perform their own spectacular fishing dives. After sighting a fish from high above the water, and setting their wings, they rocket down to the water, where they displace six feet of spray.

These family breakups may occur any time from early summer, as in shorebirds, to the following spring, as in the close-knit geese and swans. Most bird families separate following the postnuptial and post-juvenal molts of late summer when the battered nesting feathers are renewed for migration to warmer climes.

XIV Flocking

In late June, when other birds are still carrying worms to their hungry nesting young, flocks of slate-gray female cowbirds begin forming over the countryside. As each female finishes her egg-laying, she joins up with the others in her area, forming the earliest flocks of the season. Walking humorously around on their longish legs, waddling from side to side, each follows the rest of the flock in an aimless direction, picking up weed seeds and insects, exchanging incessant gurgling signals, until nightfall. Then these aberrant mothers leave the ground, fly up over the woods and coast down onto the marsh where they pass a month of nights before being joined by their fully fledged young.

When the fierce competition of nesting is over, birds revert to their normally gregarious natures and hasten to form flocks. These are of many types, ranging from the throngs of deserted young, through haphazard assemblies of various species, to the compact family units of geese and swans. Whatever type of flock gathers, the function is probably the same—sociable survival.

Birds in flocks may have fewer enemies than those in solo. Starvation is less likely to overcome them—thousands of eyes see more food than just a few, and myriad snapping bills confuse and trap more insects than could be had by one or two. Predation is restricted to the periphery, as hawks ignore a mob and pursue only lagging stragglers.

The survival value of flocking is such that Arctic-nesting redpolls desert their late nests in order to join their flocking friends. The harsh Arctic environment leaves little room for deviatory behavior—the birds must act together and well within the limits of their temperature tolerance to avoid fatal temperature drops. Consequently, the starved and frozen bodies of tiny young that had been suddenly deserted are sometimes found in their cold-stiffened willow cradles.

Some flocks consist of first-brood young pushed out of their homes by their multibrooded parents. These birds find consolation in banding with other young. Starlings flock in the vines where they hatch and Redwing young gather in the marshes, where they are joined by the adults as soon as nesting is over.

Other birds regularly leave their families in order to flock with other deserters, some of whom seem to have valid reasons, such as an excessively long molt. Cowbirds have no pressing family concerns after the eggs are laid, so they flock near and in marshes where they await the arrival of the young. Redwing males prefer to spend the nights with other males while their various mates care for the young.

Male ducks desert their mates as soon as incubation is under way. They form flocks that disappear into the marshes for the long summer molt. The nuptial plumage is shed and is replaced by a drab plumage that helps conceal the drake while he is flightless. A second molt begins in September when his new wing feathers are in.

The drab garb is pushed out by the colorful winter and prenuptial coat.

Shorebirds nesting in the Arctic form flocks for the trip south. The adults go first. The deserted young flock together for another month of growth before they migrate as a youth group.

The majority of birds flock after nesting to form large groups of intermingling families. Swallows form immense groups of both the segregated and mixed varieties. Purple Martins are the largest swallows—twelve of whom would weigh approximately one pound—and flock with thousands of their own kind. Tree Swallows also keep to themselves as a rule, forming gigantic July flights that wheel over the marshes until October, when they depart for points south. The more colorful Cliff and Bank Swallows are more compatible and flock together during late July through September.

Certainly the noisiest of these family flocks are those that combine the unfortunate voices of Starlings, Redwings, and cannibalistic grackles. These murmurations can number in the hundreds of thousands, and pass dramatically from marsh or urban roost to upland forage between July and October.

In early July, the Purple Grackle and Redwing males form their own flocks, which merge for feeding with the flocks of females and young after the August molt. The Rusty Blackbird is much more serene and does not associate with his more raucous cousins unless he is joined by them, which often happens. Bobolinks are other blackbirds who keep to their own company, congregating in the marshes for the July-August molt. They leave for Argentina on a mid-August night in order to reach southern grainfields before their more aggressive kin arrive.

Warblers seem to be the most sophisticated flockers. With great delicacy they gather in bushes and treetops only to be casually joined by flycatchers, bluebirds, chickadees, and many other unrelated species who happen to be going their way. No noise accompanies their sociability, only a gauze of whispy squeaks and the flickering of active wings.

Game birds form ghostly quiet flocks primarily as protection against winter. Quail gather in bevies that tolerate up to thirty members, roosting in protective thickets within walking distance of a berry-and-leaves food supply. The Willow Ptarmigans flock to move off the Arctic tundra into sheltered thickets, where they find protection from storm winds and can feed on wind-blown willow tips. Pheasants form bands that are strong enough to wander in search of protective roosts and ample supplies of wild fruits and seeds. Turkey families separate to flock, the gobblers banding together in small flocks, and the females and young in larger ones. They roost in dense pines near berries and leaves, the young staying with their mothers until the following spring.

Sandhill Cranes nest in the wildest solitude, then gather gregariously afterward. Canada Geese and Whistling Swan families come together as soon as the undersized young are able to fly and enter the social group. The young are bound to their parents for the first year, during which they attain adult size. In addition to the family unit there may be members of a different generation, or even a pair who have lost their young. These birds flock from September to October, their numbers being from seven or eight into the hundreds, white birds massed in maneuverable numbers, flocking to live to better advantage throughout the approaching winter and wanderlust.

XV Fall Migration

It is fall. Summer has weakened and is slipping reluctantly down the hillsides, retreating before the slow steady advance of winter. High above the gnarled trees the wind is racing past, bringing from the north the chilly currents that tumble like ice into the woods below. Still catching the early morning sunshine is one depression in the mountainside. Regularly it has been a haven for small migrating birds exhausted by flying through the predawn darkness.

Early today there seemed to be no birds. Not a stir. Nor a sound. The hollow was electric—a stillness surrounded by anxiety. And walking through, I paused to wonder why.

Swiftly the answer rose on wings. Floating at the treetops the birds appeared like a great black cloak. Twenty-five small hawks hovering with wings outspread, some motionless, others flapping to stay aloft. For seconds they dangled there, silently taking flight positions, turning their heads, exchanging looks until the group seemed ready.

Suddenly the first hawk flicked his feathered wrists to catch a passing air stream. It carried him, swift and motionless, up over a rooftop, beyond the highest trees, and out of sight. The others followed without a wingbeat. They were gone with the wind to the south.

And the small birds came out of hiding.

So a flock of hawks starts out on one of the most spectacular and least known of bird movements—the fall hawk migration. Gliding on the updrafts along the mountain ridge, they ride from thermal to thermal, gaining altitude as they ascend each chimney to the jetstream flowing southward, ever-circling, occasionally flapping their wings, until at the top some three thousand feet up they set their wings and are carried south. Hundreds and thousands of hawks will pick up the stream all along the Appalachian ridge, each entering at a thermal on the interstate flowway to the sunny south.

One mid-September day an Osprey, or Fish Hawk, was sighted coming in low on updrafts next to the hawk lookout in Montclair, New Jersey. As he approached, someone noticed that he held something in his talons. Working into the thermal created by the west wind hitting the cliff, he banked so the sun caught and revealed his prize—a ten-inch freshly caught glittering goldfish. Resplendent, soaring on his long capable wings, the bird carried the unmarred fish in its normal swimming position as a bomber carries an underslung warhead. Slowly spiraling up the thermal, the Osprey banked and banked at increasing heights, and the periodic flash of gold grew smaller and smaller. At the top, the great black and white bird flapped his long-fingered wings, set them half closed, and rode away with his sun-struck treasure.

For all migrants, the southern migration ends the northern nesting season and takes them leisurely back to their southern playgrounds for a rest. The migration is a regular movement stretching from the end of June to December, and reaching its scarcely noticeable peak in mid-September. It appears to be a slow steady passage of scattered birds coming vaguely from the north and continuing toward approximate south. Because of late summer's static weather and the addition of juveniles trying their long-distance wings for the first time, the migration lacks the crested waves of spring movements. Except for the twittering of swallows and the incessant rasping of blackbirds, the transition from summer to winter is characterized by a mysterious and peaceful silence that allows most birds to slip past unseen.

The urge to migrate seems to be a transitory one set off by hormones and external factors such as decreasing daylight. In the fall of 1929 a large number of ducks remained in western Montana and northern Idaho where open water made food available to them. Conditions were so good that they overstayed their visit—a snowstorm with sub-zero temperatures cut off the food supply, so the birds starved and froze to death with open water and food a few hundred miles distant. The urge to move out had passed them by.

The availability of food and shelter determines to a large extent whether or not certain birds migrate. As the number of daylight hours is whittled down sliver by sliver, and cool air waxes cold, green leaves turn brown, shrivel up, and fall. With them go the insects who depend on leaves for food and shelter. This fadeout happens regularly every year. For the insect-eating birds, it means the disappearance of both food and shelter in addition to the loss of daylight in which to feed. But where insects must hibernate in northern tree bark, they thrive in southern treetops, so naturally most birds follow their needs south with the passing of insects. These birds go south the way people go south—some because they cannot survive northern winters, and others because they simply function better in a warm climate.

There are two basic types of migrants, the early and the late. The early go with the passing of the longest days. They are generally delicate birds who will have less food ahead and a long way to go. The late migrants are hardy types who leave when weather dictates. They have only a short way to go to find a winter-free food supply.

The earliest migrants are the shorebirds who leave their Arctic nests from late June to August, possibly to ease the pressure on a waning food supply. The American Golden Plover subsists mainly on insects and small crustaceans that begin to disappear as the young birds get older. Shortly after the longest days have gone, the adults leave the Arctic islands, pass to Newfoundland, and fly from there to Argentina. The twenty-four hundred miles over open water are covered in two days. Since Golden Plovers swim easily it is thought that they may drop down to the ocean for food. But in fair weather some have been sighted passing over the Antilles and Bermuda without stopping. The young migrate one month later, flying the spring migration route through the interior of the United States, and rejoin the adults for the winter.

The small flycatchers and swallows are the next to flock and migrate. They leave throughout August and are followed by swifts, Common Nighthawks, and warblers, who are mostly gone by the end of September. Some of the hardy warblers remain until October along with Tree Swallows, who eat berries and seeds which their more specialized cousins cannot do.

The September–October departure of the Redwings shows their preference for insects over seeds and grains. Robins can outstay the Redwings because of their ability to extract worms and grubs from the ground and adapt themselves to the late berries. Common Crows are even more adaptable, being able to eat almost anything eatable. Both species migrate in October and November.

Like vacationers, they seem to enjoy moving for moving's sake. Northern Robins move down to Washington, D.C., in October when the southern Robins move out of Washington down to Georgia. So Washington is never without a Robin. Crows who breed in Maine migrate south to New Jersey; those who summer in New Jersey winter in Maryland; and so on down the coast.

The Canada Goose leaves the Arctic breeding grounds in October and flies south to grain fields, seed beds and shallow water where the seed diet will be open to them for the winter. Swans feed on the leaves and roots of underwater plants and are able to stay in the north until November, when the lakes freeze over and the remaining waterfowl are forced to move south toward open waters.

From July to December, fall migration offers interesting sights to anyone aware of birdlife.

From July through September, coastal beaches, mudflats, bays, and uplands are alive with shorebirds down from their night flight lanes to feed and rest for part of the day. While dark clouds of passing flocks skim over the water on the horizon, sandpipers and plovers feed on the beaches.

Compact groups of Sanderlings rush before and after each wave, moving down the wet sand with jabbing bills submerged to catch small mollusks before they disappear beneath the sand. More wary and secretive in its habits is the lone Wilson's Plover, who stands quietly on the sand, ready to run after any organism the receding water may present to his sharp eye. Other birds scurry up and down the waterside, or stand headed into the wind preening, resting and dreaming.

Back of the beaches are the tidal bays and mud flats with their salt marshes. These shelter the long-billed godwits, curlews, and Short-billed Dowitchers, as well as the yellowlegs and smaller sandpipers. Dowitchers move slowly about in the shallows, purposefully probing the bottom with their long flexible bills, "looking" for marine worms. Yellowlegs feed near them, nervously rushing from one spot to another picking insects off the water. One Lesser Yellowlegs flew from Cape Cod to the French West Indies in six days, a nineteen-hundred-mile trip averaging 316 miles per day—a remarkable migration record.

In August the skies come alive with flocks of wheeling Common Nighthawks, swallows, and swifts feeding their way southward. Unlike most birds these fliers must feed in the air as they migrate by day and do their resting at night. Toward the end of an afternoon, swallows by the thousands begin setting down on telephone wires, their masses looking like tornadoes as they funnel down to perches that fit their tiny feet.

Tree Swallows have a rule whereby no two birds shall sit closer than six inches shoulder to shoulder. Their gregariousness causes some of the incoming members to land in the middle of a flock strung out along the wires. The curious result is that both ends of the line must shuffle away from the disturbed center in an effort to redistribute the members. As long as birds drop down to roost, the line is in constant and irregular motion, making it impossible for tired individuals to sleep more than a few seconds. This rule, ludicrous as its observance may appear, assures the birds room for speedy takeoff in the event of attack by hawks, and minimizes the danger of any bird being a straggler.

Chimney Swifts spend the night in chimneys. Like swallows, they circle the chimney from a thousand feet high, the bottom members entering the chimney and clinging to the topmost space with their sharp claws. Thus they drop in until the whole flock has covered the chimney surface, sometimes roosting two or three deep when wall space is too small to accommodate the flock. Hundreds are sometimes burned to death when an untimely furnace starts up on a chilly night.

During August and September, the woods flicker with the passing of warblers, vireos, and flycatchers, who travel by night and feed by day. Their flocks move through the forest crown and undergrowth, foraging for insects, always heading south and occasionally pausing to rest. Their spirit is leisurely and their progress steady, and in their dulled fall plumage they blend well with the paling colors of autumn.

In October, marshes buzz with the calling of Redwings coming to roost between migratory laps. At sunset, flocks numbering from a few to several thousand circle the marshes and settle down into them like a pall of dense smoke. At sunrise, groups casually lift up out of the reeds, rise into the sky, and move south like a cold front, a mile-long wave ten birds deep advancing through the air. Male Redwings finding themselves caught up in a flock of females generally drop out to wait until a flock of males comes by. Pending this, if enough males gather with the same purpose, they form their own flock and are able to move on.

In late September and October, Purple Grackles pass through woodlands where they find grubs and acorns. After an hour of sustained rest and gossip in the treetops, a whoosh of wing-whipped wind sweeps through the forest canopy. Within five minutes, the flock of several hundred are scrambling in the leaves looking for food. The sound is like a rushing mountain stream. Not a voice is heard. Suddenly one bird flies wild-eyed to a rock on the lake shore holding a huge acorn in his bill. He expects a fight but no one follows, so he is able to crack and swallow his prize in peace.

Walking through the woods in the foggy dusk, one is very likely to pass under a tree laden with sleeping Cedar Waxwings. Alas, one bird hears a step, peers down, and flees with a piercing squawk. The other fifty wake up and awkwardly follow with sleepy wings, floundering out of the tree the way a wakened person bumps into furniture in the dark. The migrants are tired, and a bullfrog croaks at the disturbance.

Or passing through a field splotched with silvery blue juniper and wine-red tupelo, or beetlebung, one might suddenly encounter a bevy of young quail. One is visible, but frozen in the attitude of concealment. Brave at first, it is not long before the half-developed crest goes up and the juvenile flies out of the grass with a desperate whirr of wings. Immediately, fourteen others burst into the air and scatter in all directions, so the enemy is left standing in a vacuum, surrounded by silent birds.

Ten breathless minutes go by. Then come the first sounds from

the young who are separated, perhaps for the first time, and feel stranded. Little ventriloquistic mewings ascend from the straw-colored grass, some from the left and others from the right, a circumference of thirty yards, but nothing can be seen.

The mother decides that the flock should gather, and starts a syncopated clucking that carries to the brood. They continue their location notes for ten minutes more, all the while drawing closer together. When the group on the right have assembled to the last sound, the journey to rejoin the others begins.

In a winding line, seven straw-colored birds softly walk along the leaves that had fallen from the gray-trunked tupelo above. They stalk with great success until one steps on a withered leaf and betrays the location of the march. They stop. And freeze again when halfway to their family. Their thin dark crests perk up when they see the pale sweater move. One careless bird acts on the "now or never" theory and suddenly leaps out of the protective grass into the air, and the would-be sights of a gunner, and flies for the grove on the left. He makes it. Three seconds later the other six make a break for it, and land with the rest of the family. In the presence of the enemy, silence is maintained . . . but the family of fifteen can be heard slipping away through the grass to the left, over in the beetlebung thicket, as they retreat to safer grounds.

Over the pine scrub and near the sand dunes, a Sparrow Hawk, Cooper's Hawk, migrating Broadwing, and Peregrine Falcon all converge at one point over the same feeding area. For a brief instant the four draw together in mid-air and exchange silent nipping parries before they part.

A flock of migrating swallows swoops low over the sand-rooted pampas grasses behind the dunes, climbs high into the sky, and wends its way south, the birds scooping up insects as they swirl.

On the dunes a Peregrine Falcon appears from out of nowhere diving straight down behind a hedge on the shore. There is a tiny scream. A flock of sandpipers come up immediately, crying constantly their small but effective alarm notes, and hurry off over the dunes, leaving behind one of their members.

Out over the water a large young Gannet appears going south. With slow wingbeats, he skims over the waves like a torpedo—the long wedge-shaped tail balancing and the solid tapered head held forward and down, searching, searching, searching.

Gray fog. Redwings trill from somewhere within. A lone katydid drags its whimpering. The Woodcock up from underfoot. The dark, damp silence.

During October and November, flocks of duck appear on the gray marsh horizon, swoosh in like jets, circle, peel off, and with feet splayed wide drop to the water and plow to a bobbing stop. There they rest and feed until the flock is again ready to go on, flying by day or night because they are independent of darkness for both safety and feeding.

Through these same days and nights fly elegant lines of huge black-necked Canada Geese whose collective honks—like hounds baying in the distance—are one of the wildest and most moving sounds in the wilderness. The goose is among the wariest and wisest of birds, his movements at times appearing to be calculated. By day their flying-wedge formations can be seen for miles coming across the glowering fall landscape, each bird with one wing flying in the air-spill of the bird ahead, each able to see what is before him and where he is going.

Periodically the "leaders" drop to the rear for a rest and the rear guard move forward to cleave the icy air. The formation does not falter. The goose is a strong flier whose voice is the oil that soothes restless waters, whose back is said to carry small birds on long flights, and whose passing assures us that northern goose ponds are icing over—that winter is coming on schedule.

It is with grim foreboding that one watches a lone young goose fly a straight and rapid course north, while a hundred feet above him pass endless platoons of his kind headed south. He seems to hear the calling of the young Red-necked Grebe who was not seized with the urge to migrate and was left behind by his family at the last minute. He sits in the middle of an Arctic lake and watches the ice close in on the dark hole he has kept open with his aimless foot-waving. The ice is within three feet of him, and he needs fifty feet of open water in order to take off. Winter will not let him go.

XVI Winter

With February ferocity winter lashes the high mountain tundra of north-central Alaska. Stretching through the Brooks Range lies stark and magnificent Anaktuvuk Pass, a glaciated gravel river bed edging up into rolling treeless plains and covered with wind-packed snow. The tundra ascends gradually to the base of the wind-blasted eroded mountainsides that surmount the Pass on both sides and end at the Arctic Plain to the north.

Down in the valley the February temperature drops to fifty below zero one day and rises to twenty below the next, each change accompanied by violent winds. Two feet of snow fall during the winter. The wind whips it into a foundation strong enough to support a man and blows it from exposed spots, uncovering browse for the few animals who live there. From early October until mid-May the lakes are covered by thick ice. Their margins open up in mid-May when the shorebirds and ducks are passing through. Until then the lakes are merely part of the immense whiteness.

One mile east of the river, up on the tundra, lies mile-long Tulak Lake buried in snow, hiding the tragedy of the ice-locked grebe who will not float free until June. Forming a gray circle in the snow is the shoreline of wind-stunted willow trees.

At six in the morning a snow-white Willow Ptarmigan bursts out of its burrow roost in the snow. Through the predawn darkness it calls to the thirty other members of its winter flock and is answered. Silently the birds reassemble for the day, walking over the snow on their feather-fringed feet. As a group they move to their feeding area at the side of the lake. There they browse from one willow to the next, snapping off the tender twigs blown bare by the wailing winds. The birds feed there until noon when, sated, they settle in the snow or perch on a willow branch to rest for an hour or two.

High up near the rocky dark cliffs two Common Ravens glide, searching for carrion, lemmings, or hare. Coming down from the cliffs a large, dark Gyrfalcon skims over the tundra looking for lemmings or ptarmigans whose flocks he may follow to their wintering grounds. A Snowy Owl perches nearly invisible on a hummock near the lake, waiting for a lemming to come up for air, or for a ptarmigan to make a condemning move.

Beneath the snow a rushing stream defies the winter cold by staying open. A wrenlike Dipper walks and dives in its icy rapids looking for insect larvae. For so long as it has food, the slate-colored bird can survive the freeze.

In the willows along the lakeside, flocks of white-faced Gray Jays move heavily and jauntily through the willow bushes. Downy Woodpeckers flit from stick to stick, tapping the surfaces, looking for hibernating insects beneath the silent bark. Pine Grosbeaks and Black-capped Chickadees, muttering tit-willow, sit huddled in the willows with their fine soft feathers erected for insulation.

By early afternoon the ptarmigans are again feeding, storing up fuel to take them through the fourteen-hour Arctic night. All afternoon the flock forages, white against the white snow, until at four it disperses. Each bird flies head-on into a new snowbank, creating a roost concealed from the fox and the wolf, with no footprints leading there. The Hoary Redpolls fly into the holes where the willows rise from the snow—less to conserve heat than to hide from the Great Horned Owl. The other birds gather in protected roosting flocks, fluff out their feathers so they look like puffs, tuck their heads under their wings to conserve heat, and drift into sleep with the black night.

To human eyes these Arctic birds would appear to suffer from cold when they pull in their heads and shiver. But as long as they have plenty of food and shelter from the wind they can survive the bitter conditions of their winter resort, for they are partly adapted to winter in the far north.

Eskimos say that birds eaten in the winter are much fatter than those taken in the summer. Then the food they eat goes to insulation rather than energy for caring for the young. Birds such as the Pine Grosbeak and Hoary Redpoll have extremely fine feather tips which, when the feathers are erected, hold more heat than the feathers of more southerly birds. Substantial as these facts may seem, the most important adaptations are found in the behavior of all birds.

To survive anywhere, all birds move to areas where they can best tolerate the weather. The Glaucous Gull winters on the north Arctic shores. Like Man Bahadur of Tibet he has a heat-transferal system in his fatty legs whereby the body stays warm while the feet are cold. As the gull stays north of the mountains, the small birds must winter south of them. Large birds can be sedentary because they have a larger surface-to-volume ratio that reduces heat loss. The difference between small and large birds is similar to that between thin and fat people—one loses heat as fast as it produces it, while the other produces heat faster than it loses, just as a small radiator gives off less heat with more effort than a large one. In order to maintain their body temperature, small birds are constantly active, like small people. Beyond these basic adaptations, northern birds show no obvious differences from the southern ones.

The Eskimo who feasts on a fat ptarmigan in winter must realize the physical goodness to be derived from rest. Winter is the time when birds recuperate from the strains of the past summer, and build up for the next. Their living pattern is basically eat and sleep. What they do in between varies from bird to bird, as one bird's idea of rest may differ from that of another. The Arctic Tern flies eleven thousand miles from the Arctic to Africa to the Antarctic for his vacation, evidently valuing continuous daylight and activity. The more sedentary starling stays in the back yard the year round, possibly preferring the security of a familiar roost and food supply to long daylight. Where birds winter depends also on where their food can be found.

Large hawks and owls who live on mice and rabbits are able to stay in the frozen north. Seed-eaters, such as the finches, can winter where seeds remain relatively free of snow. Berry- and fruit-eaters, such as Robins, usually winter in southern swamps. The insect-eaters retire to the Caribbean area and South America in order to eat well.

Snowy Owls habitually winter in the Arctic where they subsist mainly on mice and lemmings. Every few years hordes of lemmings die, forcing the owls to migrate south to the United States where they live on mice.

Early in the fall of 1960 Snowy Owls began appearing in the United States, suggesting a late-summer decrease of lemmings. That winter witnessed an unusual abundance of Red-tailed and Rough-legged Hawks over the Canadian border area, indicating that the lemming population had peaked during the previous summer when the young were being raised. The hawks had converged to feed on an overabundance of field mice who were playing in the wake of a rabies epidemic that nearly eliminated the mouse-eating foxes.

Redwings winter where weeds are exposed in the winter. Although it has been estimated that they would consume sixteen billion cankerworm larvae in four months, their diet is almost one hundred percent weed seeds during the winter. The largest concentrations of these birds are found on the coastal plains between Delaware and Florida. One roost of two and a half million birds is located at Artificial Island on the New Jersey side of Delaware Bay.

Various blackbirds winter in this same general region, sometimes segregated into groups but usually intermixed. Ten roosts containing one million or more birds are known to exist in the coastal states. The largest of these is located in the Dismal Swamp near Norfolk, Virginia, where phragmites and cordgrass marsh offer seed and shelter to the fifteen million birds who winter there.

Canada Geese live primarily on the seeds and shoots of all sorts of crops. Although they concentrate during the winter mainly along the east coast, they can be found throughout the United States.

The Hairy Woodpecker is an insect-eater equipped to unbury food from its hibernating quarters beneath tree bark. But it also eats seeds. One bird found a seed box put up to take birds through the winter. While most of the birds were taking seeds from the front of the box, the woodpecker drilled away on the back. Finally after three days of labor, he broke through to the food supply, grabbed a seed in his bill and flew off with it. From then on he took seeds from the back while all the others went to the front.

Wintering birds feed all day so that they will have food to last them through the long winter nights. At sundown they return to their roosts where they settle for the night.

Most birds prefer to roost in a shelter similar to that in which they were born. Small birds roost low down in the protective bushes, while the larger bulky ones, such as crows and owls, roost high up in a swaying tree. Ptarmigans in the Arctic roost in the snow, which is where many of them hatched. Robins roost in the low bushes of secluded swamps, and Redwings in the reeds of the gaseous marshes. Hole-nesters roost in cavities and English Sparrows in crannies and vines. One enterprising sparrow passed a New York winter roosting on top of a porch light, heated from below and sheltered above. For all we know this sage may have been born there. Bobwhites huddle in a circle on the ground with their tails together and the heads pointed out. If surprised, they burst out of the circle, thereby startling and confusing the enemy and escaping into the darkness.

A large roosting area sometimes contains thousands of birds and is well worth a visit. One such roost in Florida offers entertainment to thousands of vacationers every winter.

The herons and White Ibis return to their roost from daytime feeding forays in groups of all sizes, starting about forty-five minutes before sundown. On quiet evenings they fly slowly over the marsh, head straight for the mangrove roost, alight gracefully on the branches, and walk into their favorite roosting spot.

But on windy nights the homecoming is animated. The birds come in on the wind high above the roost. Headed into the wind, they hang over the roost without flapping a wing, a flat cloud of several hundred birds, white wings outspread, red bills and faces looking down, around, and ahead. Suddenly the birds begin to peel off, clapping the air with their wings as they drop vertically through it toward the ground, and swoop up above the water to alight on the branches. Caught up with the excitement of the weather they run into the roost interior. Stepping on the feet of birds already there, an individual may lose his balance and poke a supporting wing into someone else's side, and generally create a disturbance. At first the roost is quiet as the tired birds land far apart, keeping the silence of the weary. But as more come in, the space becomes limited and voices are inevitably raised. Like other animals, birds are stimulated by one another.

As the roost fills up, the noise becomes appalling. There is constant movement among the branches—some birds land by mistake in the midst of the wrong party and objections are quickly raised. Others seem bored with their own homes and climb around in search of something better. Constant chatter is punctuated by periodic shrieks and shouts.

As the sun goes down, the visiting birds meander back to their own roosts, the hubbub settles, and for a while family talk can be heard—quiet murmurings. With the fall of darkness, all talk ceases. Quiet reigns. Only little voices can be heard every once in a while —birds talking in their sleep, or requesting that a misplaced foot be removed from the top of a weary head. All through the night discussions and squabbles take place, each reminding the rest of the world that live beings are there, but sleeping.

Robins usually roost in swamps. But an unusual event occurred at a Florida motel one evening in January. When the parking lot was nearly filled with southbound Cadillacs, a wheel of Robins high in the sky began corkscrewing down to earth, thousands of birds heading for the motel. Within minutes they were settled on all the available surface of every car in the lot. People who wished to drive to dinner attempted to scare the birds off their cars, but to no avail, as they were packed solidly together in the aftermath of a party. There they passed the night in a stupor, apparently having had their fill of an intoxicating purple berry whose remains were left on the cars when the birds departed in the morning.

Unusually harsh winters inevitably lock off the food supply of many birds, causing hibernal migrations and death. The year 1961 was heralded by a Pennsylvanian Mockingbird who burst into song over a snow-covered field in the cold light of the full moon. Able to eat wild fruits, this southern songster could still sing.

Nineteen days later the northeast entered a period of time when the temperature in Boston averaged fourteen degrees for sixteen days and was accompanied by high winds and deep snow. On January 19 a blizzard covered most ground food sources with twelve inches of snow and brought zero temperatures and winds to cut through the warmth of insulating feathers. On February 4 the temperature rose to thirty-two degrees but was accompanied by another fourteen inches of snow. Hardest hit of all birds were the ground feeders who did not regularly visit feeding stations but depended instead on the food beneath the snow.

Rivers, estuaries, and coastal bays froze up, depriving waterfowl of the aquatic vegetation growing in the shallows. Starting January 19, immense flocks of Brant, Canada, and Snow Geese moved south to the mid-Atlantic coast, and Whistling Swans departed Chesapeake Bay for the Atlantic coast. Emergency feeding operations were carried out in Nova Scotia, Maine, and Massachusetts to save thousands of birds who failed for one reason or another to move out. Nova Scotians opened up shore ice to free the eelgrass, and grain was given to twelve hundred geese who were huddling on the ice on the brink of starvation. Less than a dozen died.

On Fisher's Island, New York, the Carolina Wren was put to a severe test from which it may never recover there. From an estimated total of fifty pairs, the population over the winter dropped to "at least one" individual.

However a bright note appeared in Newfoundland where hundreds of Robins overwintered to feed on the excellent crop of Mountain Ash berries which are blessedly snow-proof.

While the birds in the south dilly-dally in the warm sunshine and food-laden bushes, the small birds in the north feel in February that spring is tentatively tiptoeing in. As the temperature climbs up from the twenties toward the low thirties, and the days start getting longer, the pattern of living begins to lose its surface anxiety.

Small sparrows, nuthatches, chickadees, and woodpeckers let leisure creep into their daytime hours. Between feedings they take more time to sit in the noonday sun, stretching their necks, shaking their feathers, flexing their feet, and looking pleasantly around to

see who else is in their tree. Warm and gay, they fly in and out of trees, filling the still crisp air with silent curtains of displaced snow.

While these small animals huddle through the cold February nights, the Great Horned Owl calls into the wild woods of his domain. *Hoo-huhoo-hoo-hoo* carries on the wind to the ears of his mate, who has lived free and alone since the previous spring when the owl family broke up. This call starts a nocturnal midwinter courtship that terminates in the end of February when the female settles down to incubate her two large eggs. By the end of March, when hares are mad and most birds are beginning to migrate, she suddenly has a family to brood through late snowstorms, winds, and rain. Through all this the owlets eat their weight in mice and rabbits each night. With the help of her mate the end of twelve weeks brings independence for the young and separation for the adults.

The bird year has been circumscribed for one hundred and thirty million years. Of these, man has shared only the last minikin million. The bird brain is still unable to make decisions—the group survives on earth because of its ability to adapt to the slow changes of nature. Instinct has been their guide, and nature their provider.

But since the supremacy of man has become a sometimes-grim reality, birds have been dying out at an unnaturally rapid rate. Because man has a brain, which often squashes his spirit and obscures his real needs, he can overnight effect changes in his environment that nature would have taken years to perform. The changes are so rapid that much of wildlife has succumbed like fish out of water, being unable to adapt on command.

Over the centuries man has "used" nature to make money, has deprived wildlife of its needs, and only now is putting pennies back into the bank. In altering the ancient course of nature to suit his own immediate purposes, man has anthropocentrically neglected the rest of his environment of which he is but a part. The current population explosion threatens to demolish it entirely.

A salmon bougainvillea in Florida was covered with luxuriant green leaves which were the hunting ground of many warblers for weeks prior to its blooming season. Suddenly a noisy and frantic family came into the house. The birds, unable to bear the traffic, shouting, and door-slamming at their feeding place, disappeared.

At the end of two weeks the vine was stripped of its leaves and even the bark was yielding to the insects. The family moved out and the birds returned to feast. Every day they picked the vine clean, until three weeks later the leaves were back and the former sticks laden with unchewed bunches of blossom. The family who had moved out were unaware of the vine and its fate, but the owners suddenly became conscious of their practical need for birds.

Aside from the practical, civilizations from the beginning of recorded time have expressed a reverence for birds. Of these, probably the most worshipped has been the eagle. Yet in these specialized times the Bald Eagle appears to be dying out from lack of consideration—and money, for the eagle cannot buy his tree.

Once-wild New Jersey produced in 1961 one young Bald Eagle. Florida, the eagle state, recorded 392 eagles. Excluding Alaska the United States census was 3576 Bald Eagles most of whom are thought to be old birds.

The probable reasons for the decline are varied. Hurricanes unfortunately come about the time that eagles are returning to Florida from the north and preparing to lay eggs. Like many other birds, and animals of all kinds, severe storms upset the eagles so that when they lay eggs at all they are likely to be sterile.

Many migrants return to find their nests taken over by the Great Horned Owl, the eagle's only serious rival in life. Because of the indiscriminate cutting of trees, the eagles often have no other tree to nest in. Then the pair will forgo the nesting season rather than leave the area to search for a new tree. Some conservationists are buying eagle trees in an effort to save them from cutting. But the good is undone when timbering around such trees exposes them to future storm winds. Others postpone building operations near eagle trees until winter when the young eagles are old enough to get along on less care.

But the main curse on eagles is the human bulldozer. The decline in Florida dates from the sudden development of the west coast after World War II. This area was wild, had a seemingly endless supply of tall strong nesting trees, and was near good fishing waters. When the trees were felled and the waters filled to support motels, restaurants, and other superabundant badges of the tourist trade, some of the eagles moved to central Florida and started a new population. Of thirty-five nests studied there in 1961, nesting success in outlying areas was sixty-five percent, and near human habitations, six percent. Eagles cannot function while humans are within one hundred and fifty to three hundred yards of the nest. They spend so much time worrying that they are unable to give the young the time and care they need.

As the American Indian retreated before westward expansion, so now the eagle is escaping human disturbance on land that is often lacking in trees and far from fishful waters—land at present thought unsuitable for human habitation, but which in all probability will be converted by bulldozers at incredible expense. However, so long as the Everglades National Park resists hostile pressure, these white-headed thunderbolts will be seen clinging to the tops of their lofty and priceless trees.

The Bald Eagle is our national symbol today. How symbolic of the democratic trend is the fact that he is in danger of extinction. In years hence how sad it would be if urbanized Americans looking at the Great Seal of the United States were to gaze not into the courageous eye of the eagle but onto the apathetic red eye of the lazy Domestic Pigeon. No more would Man hear the defiant fierce scream of the eagle calling his mate, only the incessant gurglings of these common imports, crowding the pavements and waiting for charitable handouts.

Shall Man be like the unthinking gunner who, wanting to hear the song of the dying swan, shoots a resplendent migrant out of the sky? The white bird nobly sets its wings and plummets earthward, pouring out the haunting swansong until it hits the water and is silent. The bereft man comes to appreciate its beauty only through its passing.

Appendixes

Appendix A

Some readers of the first edition of this book queried the swansong mentioned on the last page of the text. None other than the venerated Arthur Cleveland Bent reported in his classic work:

> The old saying that a swan sings before it dies has generally been regarded as a myth, but the following incident, related by so reliable an observer as Dr. G. Elliott (1898), is certainly worthy of credence:
> "I had killed many swan and never heard aught . . . save the familiar notes . . . But, once, when shooting in Currituck Sound . . . a number of swan passed over us at a considerable height. We fired at them, and one splendid bird was mortally hurt. On receiving his wound the wings became fixed and he commenced at once his song, which was continued until the water was reached, nearly half a mile away . . . Most plaintive

in character and musical in tone, it sounded at times like the soft running of the notes in an octave, and as the sound was borne to us, mellowed by the distance, we stood astonished, and could only exclaim, 'We have heard the song of the dying swan.' " [1]

The fact that few of us have heard the swansong does not necessarily mean it is a myth!

In the same vein was the report from a scientific news sheet in late 1974. It seems to be common knowledge in southern Europe that during migration small birds ride the backs of larger ones. As exceedingly few have witnessed this phenomenon, it also has been professionally debunked as myth.

In the fall of 1974, it was reported, a hunter in our midwest shot a goose, and upon retrieving the bird, discovered a live hummingbird nestled deep in the feathers of the back, invisible to the casual observer.

As the goose is a slower less proficient flyer than the hummingbird, it would not be difficult for the small bird to burrow in should the opportunity arise. But as most small birds winter much farther south than the geese it seems likely they could migrate only a short distance in such style! Be that as it may, a rarely witnessed event would better stimulate our sense of wonder than reinforce our doubtful ignorance.

Appendix B

Fledgling Florida Scrub Jays remain in the parental nest territory and assist in raising the young of the following year. Moreover, many two-year old birds do not breed, but assist in raising more families, sometimes other than those of their own parents. [2]

This interesting item reporting avian altruism gives substance to Dr. Edward O. Wilson's theory that:

In a Darwinist sense . . . the organism does not live for itself. Its primary function is not even to reproduce other organisms; it reproduces genes and serves as their temporary carrier. [3]

1. Bent, Arthur Cleveland. *Life Histories of North American Wild Fowl.* United States National Museum Bulletin 130, p. 288.8. Washington, D.C.: 1925. Reprinted by Dover Publications.
2. Woolfenden, Glen E., "Nesting and Survival in a Population of Florida Scrub Jays," *The Living Bird*, 1973.
3. Rensberger, Boyce, "Sociobiology: Updating Darwin on Behavior," *The New York Times*, May 23, 1975.

Appendix C

Birds are excellent meteorologists. In the spring they move . . . when the winds are from the south, the temperature is rising, and the barometric pressure is falling; . . . heavy fall migrations occur on nights characterized by north winds, falling temperatures, and rising air pressure.[4]

How birds navigate is still coming to light. Experiments have now demonstrated that pigeons can differentiate between minute changes in barometric pressure, a sensitivity that would be particularly useful to nocturnal flyers and those using thermal updrafts. They are also able to "detect the plane of polarized light," an ability useful to diurnal flyers seeking to determine sun direction on days of partial overcast. In addition, bar magnets have brought to light the significance of magnetic references in the flight of young and older birds alike.

The old idea that birds use a single method to determine the home direction has given way to the realization that there are probably multiple components in the system and that these components may be combined in a variety of ways, depending on such factors as weather conditions, the age of the bird and the bird's experience.[5]

Appendix D

Dr. Jurgen Nicolai at the Max Planck Institute for Behavioral Physiology at Seewiessen, Germany heard in 1972 a Purple Grenadier produce the contact trill of the Strawtailed Widow Bird. As these species inhabit the same area in Africa, Nicolai inferred and later confirmed that the imitative grenadier parasitizes the widow bird's nest.

Though the contact trill is learned as an identifying call in the forest, the begging cry used by the parasitic hatchling to assure immediate feeding by its foster parents is inborn: this cry each parasitic species has evolved to correspond to that of the host.

Moreover, it was reported, Nicolai:

has found that the intruding species has evolved an appearance in its infancy that makes it almost indistinguishable from the unwitting host. . . . immediately after the parasites hatch even the interior of the gaping, hungry mouths . . . with red maw, flanked by purple spots and

4. *Cornell Laboratory of Ornithology Newsletter* #72, Spring 1974.
5. Keeton, William T., "The Mystery of Pigeon Homing." *Scientific American,* December 1974.

fringed with scraggly hair—is shaped and colored like that of their legitimate nestmates.

Unlike the cuckoo these parasites do not throw out the eggs of the host and, hence, do not harm the widow birds except in making them work harder in their search for food.[6]

6. *The New York Times*, July 9, 1972, p. 60.

Sources and
Recommended Reading

In 1957 when I was asked to organize materials to complete the Biology of Birds Hall at the American Museum of Natural History, a wealth of professional ornithological literature was already available. My personal indoctrination began with a basic text that provided background for all else I was to observe and read:

Wallace, George J., *An Introduction to Ornithology*, (2nd Edition). New York: Macmillan, 1963.

Also used as constant references were the volumes of:

Bent, Arthur Cleveland (and collaborators). *Life Histories of North American Birds* originally published by the U.S. National Museum and now reprinted by Dover, New York.

Kendeigh, S. C., *Parental Care and Its Evolution In Birds.* Illinois Biol. Monog., 1952.

In addition to these sources I drew heavily from research papers in the professional quarterly journals, notably *The Auk, The Condor, The Wilson Bulletin,* and *The Atlantic Naturalist.*

Several dozen specialized classics greatly enriched the exhibits with their detailed information. Providing particularly pleasurable hours of learning were:

Armstrong, E. A., *The Wren.* London: Collins, 1955.

Friedmann, H., *The Cowbirds.* Springfield: Thomas, 1929.

Lack, David, *The Life of the Robin,* Fourth Edition. London: Witherby, 1965.

Nice, M. M., *Studies in the Life History of the Song Sparrow,* New York: Trans. Linnaean Soc. 1937 and 1943. (Reprinted by Dover).

Tinbergen, Niko, *The Herring Gull's World.* London: Collins, 1953. (Anchor)

The more recent literature includes a useful bimonthly journal published by the National Audubon Society in collaboration with the U. S. Fish and Wildlife Service, *American Birds*; and a quarterly, *Bird-Banding,* from the Northeastern Bird-Banding Association.

The new ecological approach is stressed in:

Lack, David (and collaborators). *Ecological Adaptations for Breeding in Birds.* London: Methuen, 1968.

Dorst, Jean, *The Life of Birds.* New York: Columbia, 1975.

Attractive to layman and professional alike are the highly diversified works issuing from the Laboratory of Ornithology at Cornell University, Ithaca, New York. In addition to their well-known sound recordings, the Laboratory annually presents *The Living Bird,* a collection of research papers amply illustrated with color photographs, drawings, and paintings by contemporary bird artists and illustrators.

For home study the Laboratory introduced in 1972 their college-level course, *Seminars in Ornithology.*

A major college text is:

Pettingill, Olin Sewall, Jr. *Ornithology in Laboratory and Field.* Minneapolis: Burgess, 1971.

This large manual could serve as *the* book necessary to the pursuit of bird study in armchair or field. Not only does each chapter end with a list of references drawn from the works of the world, but so do sections within chapters. In addition, a 78-page bibliography divided into life history studies (14 pages), regional works (18), general recreational reading (6), and ornithological journals (6) seems to cover the entire scope of ornithological literature from the United States and Argentina east to Hawaii and Japan. Developed over thirty-four years this work provides an extraordinary learning tool in the field of ornithology.

Among the many books available for young and adult readers I recommend for their accuracy and poignancy Griffing Bancroft's three highly informative life stories, each complete with suggested reading list:

Snowy, the Story of an Egret. New York: McCall, 1970.
Vanishing Wings, A Tale of Three Birds of Prey. New York: Watts, 1972.
The White Cardinal. New York: Coward McCann, 1973.

Until now most ethological studies have been used by other behavioral students. Now they are providing input to a broader sociobiological picture, being drawn by a new group of scientists, who are integrating the descriptive reports of behavioral research with the tenets of Darwinian theory. A definitive volume on their work is:

Wilson, Sr., Edward O., *Sociobiology, the New Synthesis.* Cambridge: Harvard, 1975.

Dr. Wilson suggests among other things that man's drive toward social perfection may represent a genetic determination that originated among our animal ancestors.

Index